Praise for *Data Quality Engineering in Financial Services*

This book is an essential reading not only for the data management specialists but for anyone who works with and relies on data. Brian Buzzelli harnesses his many years of practical, "been there, done that, have scars to prove it" experience to teach the reader how to apply manufacturing quality control principles to "find a needle in a haystack"—that one erroneous attribute that will have an outside impact.

—*Julia Bardmesser, SVP, Head of Data, Architecture and Salesforce Development, Voya Financial*

This is the perfect playbook that, if implemented, will allow any financial services company to put their data on an offensive footing to drive alpha and insights without sacrificing quality, governance, or compliance.

—*Michael McCarthy, Principal Investment Data Architect, Investment Data Management Office, MFS*

The approach to data quality expressed in this book is based on an original idea of using quality and standardization principles applied from manufacturing. It provides insights into a pragmatic and tested data quality framework that will be useful to any data practitioner.

—*Predrag Dizdarevic, Partner, Element22*

This book clearly explains how to apply a manufacturing approach to data quality, provides an easy framework to capture data quality requirements, and has high-impact data quality metrics and visualization.

—*Alag Solaiappan, VP, Data Engineering, Acadian Asset Management*

This book is a must for any data professional, regardless of industry. Brian has provided a definitive guide on how to best ensure that data processes—from sourcing and ingestion, to firmwide utilization—are properly monitored, measured and controlled. The insights that he illustrates are born out of a long history of working with content and enabling financial professionals to perform their jobs. The principles presented herein are applicable to any organization that needs to build proper and efficient data governance and data management. Finally, here is a tool that can help everyone from chief data officers to data engineers in the performance of their roles.

—*Barry S. Raskin, Head of Data Practice,*
Relevate Data Monetization Corp.

Brian Buzzelli presents a clear how—to guide for the finance professional to motivate, design, and implement a comprehensive data quality framework. Even in early stages, the data quality program will improve efficiency, reduce risk, and build trust with clients and across functions. Brian demonstrates the connection between data integrity and fiduciary obligation with relevant examples. Borrowing unabashedly from concepts in high precision manufacturing, Brian provides a step-by-step plan to engineer an enterprise level data quality program with solutions designed for specific functions. The code examples are especially applicable, providing the reader with a set of practical tools. I believe these concepts are an important contribution to the field.

—*Matthew Lyberg, CFA, Quantitative Researcher, NDVR Inc.*

Data Quality Engineering in Financial Services
Applying Manufacturing Techniques to Data

Brian Buzzelli

Beijing · Boston · Farnham · Sebastopol · Tokyo

Data Quality Engineering in Financial Services

by Brian Buzzelli

Copyright © 2023 Brian Buzzelli. All rights reserved.

Published by O'Reilly Media, Inc., 1005 Gravenstein Highway North, Sebastopol, CA 95472.

O'Reilly books may be purchased for educational, business, or sales promotional use. Online editions are also available for most titles (*http://oreilly.com*). For more information, contact our corporate/institutional sales department: 800-998-9938 or *corporate@oreilly.com*.

Acquisitions Editor: Michelle Smith	**Indexer:** Potomac Indexing, LLC
Development Editor: Corbin Collins	**Interior Designer:** David Futato
Production Editor: Beth Kelly	**Cover Designer:** Karen Montgomery
Copyeditor: Nicole Taché	**Illustrator:** Kate Dullea
Proofreader: Shannon Turlington	

October 2022:   First Edition

Revision History for the First Edition

2022-10-19:   First Release

See *http://oreilly.com/catalog/errata.csp?isbn=9781098136932* for release details.

978-1-098-13687-1

[LSI]

Table of Contents

Preface

Most people would say we live in a world where we trust in the manufacturing discipline and quality standards used to provide the food we eat, the water we drink, the medications we take, and the sophisticated technology products we use in our daily lives. We can appreciate the years of evolution in science, refinement in manufacturing techniques, and codification of product specifications that form the basis of the trust we enjoy in consuming and using physical products today. Given the monumental achievements in science, technology, and manufacturing; what then is so different about the data used in the financial industry whereby data and information must be constantly checked, rechecked, and reconciled to ensure its accuracy and quality?

Data is the fundamental raw material used in the financial industry to manage your retirement and family's wealth assets, provide operating and growth capital to companies, and drive the global financial system as the life blood of the global economy. Unlike the manufacturing industry, data flows in the financial industry have evolved from being based on open outcry, telephone, paper trails, and ticker tapes, to being grounded in sophisticated and complex computational, artificial intelligence, and machine learning applications. We capture, store, and pass along data through complex applications, and we use data in business processes with a general assumption that the data is reliable and suitable for use.

However, data has no physical form and has the capacity to be infinitely malleable. By contrast, the raw materials in manufacturing have physical form. The physical properties can be measured and assessed for suitability based on the specification for the physical properties and tolerances for which the raw material is certified compliant for use. This is one of the key concepts whereby we will apply a similar manufacturing framework to data and define the properties of data that can be measured against a specification. Examples of data will be presented as if it has mass and physical form, but in the context of measurable data dimensions: completeness, timeliness, accuracy, precision, conformity, congruence, collection, and cohesion.

The premise in this book is that data has shape, has measurable dimensions, and can be inspected and measured relative to data quality specifications and tolerances that yield data quality metrics. The results can then be analyzed using data quality specifications to derive data quality metrics. The data quality processes in manufacturing include evaluating specific measurements of physical materials relative to control specifications. The results are analyzed to determine whether the materials quality measurements and metrics are within design specifications and acceptable tolerances.

While the financial industry struggles with a lack of industry standards for data identification, definition, and representation, combined with the fast pace of financial product innovation, manufacturing evolution and maturity demonstrates highly robust methodologies, accuracy, and purity in techniques, and precision in materials processing. Today we enjoy and perhaps take for granted the technical complexities that give us modern medicines, genetics, super crops, jets, satellites, smartphones, flat screen TVs, artificial intelligence, robotics, wristwatch computers—the list is endless.

The financial industry can learn a great deal from the application of mature manufacturing techniques to our immature data management discipline. The primary benefit of applying similar precision in data quality validations is high quality data. However, from a business perspective, additional benefits include the following:

- Operational efficiency
- Lower cost of operations
- Less wasted effort
- Higher data precision
- More accurate business decision making

This book is intended to provide useful frameworks and techniques that can be introduced into your data structures and data management operations. The expectation is the application of these techniques and frameworks will improve data processing efficiency, data identification, data quality, reduce operational data issues, and increase trust that the data is business ready and fit for purpose.

My Journey and a Brief History of Data in the Financial Services Industry

I have worked in the financial industry for 27+ years in both technical and business roles wrestling with and managing data. Over the years, early organizations such as the Data Warehousing Institute (TDWI) (*https://oreil.ly/Sphea*) and Data Management Association International (DAMA) (*https://dama.org*) have led the early focus on data and data management. Many other industries such as pharma, aerospace, and technical manufacturing have significantly advanced in physical materials quality management, and society have reaped the benefits of Lean, total quality management (TQM), Six Sigma, and so on. Comparatively, the financial industry has lagged far behind in the definition and adoption of unified data definition and data quality standards. Though the industry has employed certain standards such as the Society for Worldwide Interbank Financial Telecommunications (SWIFT), the Financial Information Exchange (FIX) protocol, International Standards Organization (ISO) country and ISO currency standards, the industry has traditionally lacked a global, common, standardized, unified data taxonomy and ontology that defines and identifies securities and investment instruments in the global financial system.

The Software Publishers Association was established in 1984 and then merged with the Information Industry Association in 1999 and was renamed the Software and Information Industry Association (SIIA) (*http://siia.net*). The Financial Information Services Division (FISD) (*https://oreil.ly/sPC0N*), a division of SIIA, was formed to focus specifically on the financial industry and primarily market data and information. At that time, more than two decades ago, most financial information revolved around the markets, and the primary distributers Reuters and Bloomberg delivered the market ticks, issuer and security information, and company fundamentals, and filings.. Generally, the equities markets used Committee on Uniform Securities Identification Procedures (CUSIP), Stock Exchange Daily Official List (SEDOL), and International Securities Identification Number (ISIN) for securities identification. As fixed income, synthetics, derivatives, and securitized products entered the financial system, and with no standardized definition nor national securities exchanges, the industry saw tremendous divergence in data definitions, valuations, identification schemes, and so on. The primary data vendors such as Reuters, Bloomberg, Interactive Data, Thomson Financial, and Telekurs were the powerhouses that provided the extended reference data and related analytics, and each had its own unique way of curating the data and packaging the data into data products. They were competitors, so the lack of industry adopted standards for interoperability/substitution combined with the lack of regulatory mandated common taxonomy hindered any major improvement in common data definition and data management practices.

Then came the rise of the enterprise data management (EDM) platforms, including Eagle PACE, Asset Control, Cadis, and GoldenSource. I have extensive experience implementing and managing Eagle PACE as well as driving data integrations to several EDM platforms. That's how I gained significant insight into data architecture, data structuring, data quality validations, data provisioning, curation, and more.

Mike Atkin, former president of the FISD, left in 2004 and formed the Enterprise Data Management Council (*https://oreil.ly/bmnMA*) in 2005 with participation from several data vendors, including Reuters. The EDM Council's initial mission focused on improving methods and frameworks for data definitions and data management practices with special emphasis on reference and analytical data. Today, the EDM Council and the Global Legal Entity Identifier Foundation (GLEIF) (*https://oreil.ly/*

E1fLl) have been exceptional leaders in driving global data management and standards initiatives to improve data management discipline in the financial industry. I have been a member of SIIA and FISD, a contributing member of the EDM Council, and an industry participatory member of the GLEIF during its formation.

Today I have had the privilege to collaborate with other industry data experts and practitioners, and collectively we have contributed to the evolution and maturity of how we define data, instruments, attributes, analytics, entities, and the like. You will now find many variations of the data dimensions frameworks illustrated by various working groups, associations, authors, vendors, and so on, but there is no common, single, agreed reference to data dimensions.

It became apparent to me that data quality is not only multi-faceted, in that it reflects the individual and combined tolerances for each dimension, but that the very individual tolerances across dimensions for each datum differ according to the target use case. Thus, I designed a data quality specification (DQS) that embodies the alignment of data dimensions, data quality tolerances and validations, and the data quality expectation of the consumer or consuming system. This definition of the DQS differs from other practitioner definitions due to its focus on a specific set of eight quantitatively measurable data dimensions, and for each data quality tolerance definition, the DQS includes the concept of suspect. This provides three main categories:

Valid
> Within tolerance

Suspect
> Approaching out of tolerance

Invalid
> Out of tolerance

This approach leads to greater delineation between within tolerance and out of tolerance conditions.

For example, consider global economic data used by quantitative researchers to understand trends and patterns versus a portfolio holdings file that contains null values in the price data element. The use case might be to generate a portfolio net asset value and return. The DQS of the data quality across the data is remarkably different for each use case, yet the datasets may commonly contain a price data element.

This book provides useful frameworks and techniques for implementing data governance, master data management, and data quality engineering. The application of manufacturing principles and techniques to data management, used in combination with these frameworks, is intended to promote structured data architectures and a more disciplined and precise data management operation, yielding higher quality fit-for-purpose data and lower operational cost and risk.

This book aims to teach you how to define, engineer, and use data validation checks and quality tolerances to deliver high quality data that meets the consumers data quality specification. The book will introduce you to data governance and the role it plays in driving best practices in data management. You will learn about manufacturing and how manufacturers use precise material and processing control specifications to ensure the physical properties of raw and semifinished materials meet the manufacturing requirements. Data in the financial industry is like the raw materials used in the manufacturing industry. You will be challenged to think about a volume of data as if it were a volume of raw material to be used in manufacturing. You will learn about the shape of data, timeseries data, cross section data, panel data volumes, and the dimensions of data. You will be able to specify precise data quality checks and tolerances at the datum level to ensure only high quality data is used that meets the consumer or application use case. You will learn how to generate data quality metrics and analytics based on standardized data quality measurements that support a consistent approach to data quality engineering. A master data management approach will be used to demonstrate the concepts of raw, staged, and mastered data provide the architecture in which you can apply the data quality engineering techniques and prevent data that does not meet the consumer data quality specification from being provisioned and used. Finally, you will see how enterprise data management is the combination of data governance, data quality engineering, and master data management.

These concepts and techniques are intertwined within the many of the tasks commonly performed across different data intensive business and technical engineering functions in the financial industry. Generally, most professionals in the financial industry are data practitioners and include business professionals, data scientists, data analysts, data engineers, and data architects. Business and technical professionals who operate in data intensive functions such as data management, data analytics, research, portfolio management, portfolio construction, trading, accounting operations, compliance, and performance measurement to name a few will benefit from these data quality frameworks. Data quality is determined by the consumer or application based on data quality specifications. The consumer can use these frameworks to convey the precise data quality tolerances about the data intended for their use or to be used by an application. The data analysts and technicians responsible for implementing data management architectures and data management processes can use these frameworks to understand the data quality requirements of the consumer and engineer data quality measurements into the data ecosystem.

You can directly apply these techniques to understanding the quality of the data you are using or about to use. The application of data quality engineering frameworks will empower you with deep insight about the shape and the quality of your data, and the ability and language to precisely convey to others the data quality required.

Conventions Used in This Book

The following typographical conventions are used in this book:

 This element signifies a tip or suggestion.

 This element signifies a general note.

 This element indicates a warning or caution.

https://oreil.ly/DQEF-figures

Online Figures

You can find larger, color versions of some figures at *https://oreil.ly/DQEF-figures*. Links to each figure also appear in their captions.

Email *bookquestions@oreilly.com* if you have a technical question.

O'Reilly Online Learning

 For more than 40 years, *O'Reilly Media* has provided technology and business training, knowledge, and insight to help companies succeed.

Our unique network of experts and innovators share their knowledge and expertise through books, articles, and our online learning platform. O'Reilly's online learning platform gives you on-demand access to live training courses, in-depth learning paths, interactive coding environments, and a vast collection of text and video from O'Reilly and 200+ other publishers. For more information, visit *http://oreilly.com*.

How to Contact Us

Please address comments and questions concerning this book to the publisher:

O'Reilly Media, Inc.
1005 Gravenstein Highway North
Sebastopol, CA 95472
800-998-9938 (in the United States or Canada)
707-829-0515 (international or local)
707-829-0104 (fax)

We have a web page for this book, where we list errata, examples, and any additional information. You can access this page at *https://oreil.ly/DQE*.

Email *bookquestions@oreilly.com* to comment or ask technical questions about this book.

For news and information about our books and courses, visit *http://oreilly.com*.

Find us on LinkedIn: *https://linkedin.com/company/oreilly-media*.

Follow us on Twitter: *https://twitter.com/oreillymedia*.

Watch us on YouTube: *https://youtube.com/oreillymedia*.

Acknowledgments

There is no "I" in the word *data*, nor in the word *success*, and the same is true for the development and production of this book, which has been made possible by the contributions and support of many. I would like to express my deepest thanks and appreciation for the professional and personal support, contributions, and encouragement I have received from Acadian, O'Reilly Media, industry colleagues, fellow data practitioners, friends, and family. The successful achievement of producing this book is to be shared by all.

I would like to recognize and thank the team at Acadian Asset Management: Executive Vice President and Chief Investment Officer Brendan Bradley, Senior Vice President and Director of Investment Analytics and Data Jim Dufort, and the incredible Enterprise Data Management and Information Technology teams for their support and commitment to the application of manufacturing principles and the continuous improvement of the firm's data architectures, data management operations, data quality validations, and data governance discipline. The frameworks and techniques provided in this book have been proven to work due to the collective and successful implementation efforts of my Acadian colleagues. I am truly grateful to them for their willingness to think differently about data quality and data management. "Acadian-ites" have embraced architectural and procedural changes that deliver high-quality data for use across the firm and that support Acadian's innate commitment to delivering exceptional investment products and client services.

My sincere thanks to O'Reilly Media: Content Acquisition Editor Michelle Smith, Content Development Editor Corbin Collins, Production Editor Elizabeth Kelly, and Copy Editor Nicole Taché. Thank you for the tremendous opportunity to bring this book to fruition. I am grateful for the privilege to contribute to O'Reilly Media's content and success. This book would not be possible without Michelle's keen insight and recognition of the importance and relevance of data quality in the financial industry. Michelle understood the foundational frameworks in this book would be helpful to all data practitioners. I cannot thank Corbin enough for his patience, expertise, recommendations, suggestions, feedback, and steady and clear guidance while working with me to develop the content in this book. My gratitude extends to Elizabeth, Nicole, Suzanne Huston, and the production team for their expertise in the preparation, presentation, and production of this book. I have a newfound appreciation and highest respect for content editors, copy editors, and publishing professionals. The exceptional expertise demonstrated by these individuals contributes to O'Reilly Media's success.

The successful development of key concepts, and the accuracy of the content and examples in this book were made possible by multiple technical reviewers. I wish to thank Predrag Dizdarevic, founder and partner of Element22, for his industry leadership, his many years of experience, and his expertise that he graciously imparted during the technical reviews of this book. My heartfelt thanks to Abdullah Karasan, PhD, senior data science consultant at TFI TAB Food Investments and author of *Machine Learning for Financial Risk Management with Python* (O'Reilly), for the deep expertise and sharp insights conveyed in his technical review. I would also like to thank fellow data quality warrior and practitioner Alagappan Solaiappan, vice president, senior data analyst, EDM data quality engineer at Acadian, for his many years of experience, his expertise in data quality, and his exceptional collaboration with me and our fellow Acadian colleagues. Data is a team sport, and his feedback and meticulous technical review of the book has contributed to its success.

I wish to recognize and thank Matthew Lyberg, CFA, quantitative researcher at NDVR, Inc. and former director of performance attribution at Acadian, for his insights and feedback that drove many improvements in the definition and demonstration of the data quality concepts and the DQS framework. His recognition of the business value embodied in this work led to my introducing it to the CFA Institute. They now include portions of this work in their training curriculum. My thanks to all data quality warriors, data practitioners, and industry colleagues who strive to deliver the highest quality data in our financial services and asset management firms.

On a personal note, my deepest thanks to Barbara Buzzelli (Mom), Richard Buzzelli (Dad), and Claudine Wagenfuehr (sister) for their love, support, and unending encouragement. Mom always said, "You can do anything you set your mind to." I *can*...and I *did*. I also wish to thank Dr. Andrew T. Revel, who is my best friend, greatest supporter, fiercest critic, and through the many years, my partner in life. My thanks to "The Foundation" that includes Robert Davis, Peggy Walther, and Chuck Wesley (IM), for their unending friendship, support, and encouragement. My thanks and appreciation to Matthew Szczepanski for his support and encouragement during the early, formative years at university and at the beginning my career. Many thanks to Nancy Pribich who gave me a *swift kick* as motivation to pursue my dreams and aspirations, and to work hard to achieve them. Finally, my recognition and gratitude for the exceptional education I received at both Carnegie Mellon University and the University of Pittsburgh, which gave me the technical foundations to develop this book, and to build and achieve my career goals.

CHAPTER 1

Thinking Like a Manufacturer

This chapter introduces concepts of efficiency, effectiveness, and Lean manufacturing along with several examples of high-quality excellence in manufacturing. Manufacturers use raw and semifinished materials to create products. Thinking like a manufacturer means thinking about data as a raw or semifinished material and thinking about data management processes much like manufacturers think about the production process in a factory. There are many similarities between manufacturing a product and managing data:

- Both use raw and semifinished materials
- Both require detailed manufacturing control specifications
- Both include quality validations and verifications
- Both use quantitative tolerances and measures to confirm conformance to a specification

Operational Efficiency

There are many definitions of *operational efficiency*, but I define it as the ratio between the inputs to run a business operation and the outputs gained from its production. Improving a business's operational efficiency means the output-to-input ratio also improves. Common business inputs typically include money, intellectual property, and employees. The business outputs typically realized include products, revenue, customers, market differentiation, productivity, innovation, and so on.

Poor data quality is one of the main contributors to operational inefficiency in the financial industry. It impacts a financial firm's ability to efficiently conduct business and it can lead to inaccurate business insights, incorrect financial analyses, and erroneous investment decisions. Further, incorrect or misaligned data negatively impacts operational efficiency whereby employees are constantly spending their time checking and rechecking data quality. Misrepresentation of financials to clients, regulators, and auditors can have severe impacts on operational effectiveness.

A firm should strive to maximize efficiency and effectiveness by ensuring only high-quality data and information are used in production data processes. Applying a manufacturing approach to data management—with precise, pre-use data quality validations—contributes to operational efficiency and effectiveness. With *pre-use data quality validations*, the quality of the data is confirmed, verified, and validated relative to DQS *before* the data is used by the consumer.

Generally, the following activities lead to a more disciplined data management operation and higher quality data used across the firm:

- Applying a manufacturing approach to data quality management
- Implementing data quality specifications (DQS)
- Implementing pre-use data validations as primary data quality controls
- Transforming reconciliations into post-use data verifications as secondary data quality controls
- Measuring the data quality of the dimensions of your data

Lessons from Lean Manufacturing

The term *Lean* was used to describe Toyota's car manufacturing business during the late 1980s. A research team, headed by Jim Womack, PhD, at MIT's International Motor Vehicle Program, began using this term in the context of manufacturing.

A Lean organization understands the essence of customer value, focuses key processes to continuously increase customer value, and creates and provides value through its processes with a zero-waste objective. A Lean organization changes its focus from optimizing separate technologies, assets, and departments to optimizing the horizontal flow of products and services through value-generating processes across technologies, assets, and departments.

A major goal of a Lean organization is to eliminate waste throughout its processes, instead of at isolated points. It endeavors to create production processes that require less capital and less human effort, and that yield fewer defects, ultimately at far less cost. The lesson from Lean manufacturing applied to data directly relates to data quality. Lean principles applied in manufacturing or an assembly line focus on eliminating waste. Similarly, thinking like a Lean manufacturer when managing data means *reducing or eliminating poor-quality data that does not satisfy DQS.*

Coca-Cola: Excellence in Manufacturing Quality

Coca-Cola is one of the largest multinational beverage producers in the world. The quality of the finished product is immensely important to satisfy consumers. However, in addition to consistently delivering the exact flavor of a beverage, the company must also apply stringent quality controls to all aspects of its manufacturing process. This is especially true for the raw materials such as flavoring, water, and containers since the beverage is human consumable. Coca-Cola provides a glimpse into the details of its quality assurance framework on its website (*https://oreil.ly/xrBIJ*), which I also summarize in this section.

Coca-Cola delivers high-quality beverage products and meets consumer expectations using precise quality measurements for ingredients, packaging, manufacturing, bottling, and distribution. All products manufactured by Coca-Cola pass through quality inspections before being released for distribution.

Quality control specialists initially check the manufacturing line before starting up the bottling process. They inspect and verify the CO_2 volumes and confirm the ratio of water-to-syrup matches the quality specifications for production. Within 30 minutes of starting the bottling process, they check the net contents to verify the proper volume is being bottled. Finally, they perform torque checks to verify the tightness of the bottle caps, and to verify that the labels on the bottles meet production guidelines.

Coca-Cola is an example of excellence in manufacturing. We generally trust in the quality and safety of its beverages because simply mixing carbon dioxide, water, and flavored syrup is not enough. Coca-Cola adheres to industry safety standards and conducts many checks and validations to ensure the quality of its finished products.

DASANI®: Purifying Water

Coca-Cola owns DASANI®, one of the world's largest purified water producers in the world. The company uses a series of sophisticated quality controls to produce potable purified water. The purification steps performed are outlined on its website (*https://oreil.ly/znBaF*) and generally include the following:

1. Volatile organic compounds and chlorine are absorbed by activated carbon filtration.

2. Minerals and additional impurities are removed by reverse osmosis.

3. Interim ultraviolet light disinfection destroys microorganisms and ensures water safety and purity.

4. Water is remineralized by the addition of small amounts of magnesium sulfate, potassium chloride, and salt to ensure consistent taste.

5. Final purification takes place using ozonation. Ozone gas, which has disinfectant properties, is pumped through the water. Because ozone, O_3, is a type of oxygen, it quickly dissipates into the same type of oxygen gas we breathe, O_2, and does not leave any residual taste in the water.

6. All steps are continually monitored and tested on a regular basis.

Refer to the DASANI® Annual Analysis Example (*https://oreil.ly/nW5VJ*) for more detailed information on the multitude of tests used to confirm that DASANI® is in compliance with water quality standards.

These two examples illustrate the high degree of quality specifications required to produce what seem to be simple beverages.

Manufacturing Control Specifications

The production of products using labor, machines, tools, chemical and biological processing, or formulation is referred to as *manufacturing*. Transformation of raw materials into finished products at scale is called *industrial manufacturing*. The research function in manufacturing focuses on improvements and innovation in both the products and the product manufacturing processes. The engineering function focuses on product design, materials specifications, and the manufacturing transformation processes. The product manufacturing processes are controlled using quality assurance plans, control specifications, and control plans.

Water Quality Specifications

Water is used in many ways, from human consumption to the production of semiconductors. Let's look at an example that illustrates dramatically different water quality specifications, and associated tolerances, for three different use cases: ultrapure water, potable water, and mineral water.

Semiconductor chip production requires ultrapure water. *Ultrapure* water, in general, only contains H_2O, a balance of hydrogen and oxygen ions, and has been purified to high levels of quality specification. Contaminants in the water used for chip manufacturing would render the production process useless.

Water for human consumption, by contrast, must meet different quality standards. *Potable* water is drinking water that is filtered and treated to quality specifications for human consumption. Biological pathogens, organic and inorganic matter, and chemical contaminants in the water are removed or may exist per standards at levels below maximum safe tolerances.

Potable water does not mean the water tastes good, but rather that it is safe to drink. The perception of good-tasting potable water has more to do with the dissolved minerals and human taste buds. Generally, *mineral* water seems to taste better to humans and often contains some combination of dissolved sodium, potassium, chloride, bicarbonate, sulfate, calcium, and magnesium. Quality in this context is defined by additional characteristics in addition to the requirements for water to be potable.

 The key concepts illustrated by these three water quality specifications are as follows:

- The same raw material can be used by more than one type of consumer and for more than one purpose.
- The quality specification of the material is defined by the consumer use case requirements.
- The quality specifications may differ dramatically across multiple consumer use cases.
- The quality of the material must satisfy the quality specification to be viable for use.

Quality Control and Anomaly Detection

Manufacturers use precise material and manufacturing control specifications. They apply quality tests to the raw and semifinished materials entering the manufacturing assembly line, and use sensors that measure tolerances of product components to assess their viability and to control production processes. In general, materials must successfully pass the quality gates *before* being moved to the next processing step.

To identify unexpected events in the manufacturing process, manufacturers use *anomaly detection* techniques, which employ signals generated from sensors and tolerance measurements. *Quality control* is a critical function that focuses on identifying anomalies and understanding their implication in the manufacturing process. This is a highly sophisticated and complex manufacturing discipline. For more on anomaly detection, consult *Anomaly Detection for Monitoring* by Preetam Jinka and Baron Schwartz (O'Reilly). For a detailed presentation of manufacturing-related metrics and analytical measurement models, see *Smart Process Plants* by Miguel J. Bagajewicz (McGraw Hill).

Summary

A manufacturing production process uses quality and control specifications to precisely define and specify the physical characteristics and quality tolerance requirements of raw and semifinished materials. The same raw materials can be used for multiple manufacturing purposes. The quality specifications of the materials are defined by the consumer use case requirements. Finally, the quality of the materials must satisfy the quality specifications for it to be viable in the production process.

Manufacturing uses control specifications much like the financial industry uses DQS to engineer data quality validations.

Like product manufacturing, data manufacturing and data quality are controlled using precise DQS. Data quality is assessed *before* the data is provisioned to downstream processes, applications, or consumers. DQS will differ depending on the different consumer use cases. Pre-use data validations prevent data that does not satisfy DQS from polluting the downstream data ecosystem.

The next chapter introduces you to the shape of data and data dimensions. It provides the conceptual framework to understand the techniques used to measure those dimensions, relative to tolerances defined in DQS. You will see how commonly used datasets in the financial industry are data volumes, composed of panel data or cross-section time series datasets. Data volumes contain records of data that include data elements or columns. Each data element is a set of individual datum. You will be able to measure the applicable dimensions of a specific datum, and for all datum in a data volume, by applying the measurement techniques and data quality tolerances defined in DQS.

CHAPTER 2

The Shape of Data

This chapter will challenge you to think like a manufacturer and to think about data as if it had physical form. This thought process, this comparison to manufacturing physical material, is the first step toward developing an enlightened understanding about data, its shape and form, and (most importantly) assessing data quality at the data dimension level.

Data as Physical Asset

In your firm, data must be thought of as a critically important physical asset. When data is treated as a physical material and regarded as an asset of the firm, then applying techniques used in industrial materials manufacturing to achieve high-quality products becomes easier to understand and implement.

Data has temporal dimensionality, which means data is generally either dynamic or persistent:

Dynamic data
> This type of data changes over time and is fluid in the context of the business processes (e.g., current analytics, trade lists, portfolio positions, transactions, cash flows, performance).

Persistent data
> This type of data does not change (at least, not nearly as much). This data represents history.

Dynamic and persistent data are managed and curated differently, and often with different technologies and techniques. Curated, fully validated, confirmed historical data typically represents persistent data.

Data lives in technology. While this seems obvious, it is important to recognize that all data initiatives require a technological component, since data does not exist without technology. The related concepts of master data management and data architecture are covered later in this book.

Data Shape Concept Model

Though data has no physical form, we can measure and assess the quality of the data using techniques applied to the dimensions that define its shape.

The *data shape concept model* is the conceptual foundation for thinking about and visualizing volumes of data used in the financial industry, like a manufacturer uses volumes of raw or semifinished materials (such as silica, water, minerals, metals, plastics, and so forth) in a manufacturing production process. The model tells us that data can have the following shapes, which we'll discuss next:

- Data element
- Datum
- Data universe
- Time series data
- Cross-section data
- Panel data
- Data volumes

Data Element

A *data element* is the smallest single named data item that has a unique definition. Examples might include close price, exchange rate, market value, and so on. A close price, for instance, is the named data element that represents the last price of a traded stock during a regular trading session.

Datum

A *datum* is a single data point value (such as $143.11) for a data element. For example, a close price could be $143.11, an exchange rate could be 0.93, a market value could be $349,292, and so on. Figure 2-1 illustrates a close price datum of $143.11.

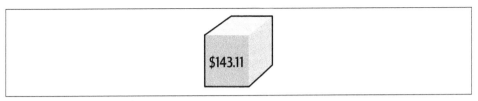

Figure 2-1. Close price datum

Data Universe

A *data universe* is a dataset of related items (such as stocks) that together form a named group called a *universe* (such as a stock universe, or a universe of issuers, a universe of stocks, a universe of currencies, and so on). Table 2-1 shows a stock universe.

Table 2-1. Stock universe

Stock
Apple
Google
IBM

Time Series Data

Time series data is a set of datums (single data point values) for a specific data element (e.g., close price) for one universe item (e.g., Apple) over multiple points in time (e.g., 05/23/22, 05/24/22, 05/25/22). Table 2-2 is an example of a close price time series dataset for Apple.

Table 2-2. Close price time series data

Stock	Close price	Date
Apple	$143.11	05/23/22
Apple	$140.36	05/24/22
Apple	$140.52	05/25/22

Time series data that has one variable or dimension (e.g., close price) is referred to as a *univariate time series*, or a longitudinal dataset that depends on time. The data can also be represented as a one-dimensional array or linear array. Figure 2-2 shows the Apple close price time series data presented in a one-dimensional array, where the close price is located on the x-axis (date).

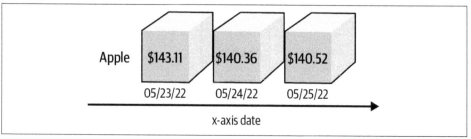

Figure 2-2. Close price time series data in array form

Thinking about a collection of data as a physical volume of raw material begins with visualizing data in your mind as if it has mass and exists in a three-dimensional space. This is an important, foundational concept that will anchor your ability to think about and use data like a manufacturer uses raw materials. Many of the concepts and frameworks—for example, data dimensions, DQS, and data quality tolerances—that follow in this book are analogous to the control specifications, quality assurance, and production control techniques that manufacturers use in their production processes.

Cross-Section Data

A *cross-section dataset* is a set of datums (single data point values) for a specific data element (e.g., close price) for multiple items (e.g., stocks) in a universe (e.g., stock universe) at one point in time (e.g., 05/23/22). Table 2-3 is an example of a close price cross-section dataset.

Table 2-3. Close price cross-section data

Stock	Close price	Date
Apple	$143.11	05/23/22
Google	$2,233.33	05/23/22
IBM	$131.17	05/23/22

Cross-section data has one variable or dimension and is therefore a univariate dataset. The data can also be represented as a one-dimensional array or linear array. Figure 2-3 shows the close price cross-section data presented in a one-dimensional array where the close price is located on the x-axis (stock).

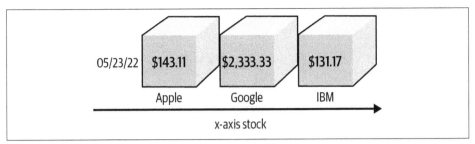

Figure 2-3. Close price cross-section data in array form

Panel Data

A *panel dataset*, or *time series cross-section*, is a combination of time series and cross-section datasets. Panel data is sets of datums (single data point values) for one or more data elements (e.g., open price, close price) for multiple items (e.g., stocks) in a universe (e.g., stock universe) over multiple points in time (e.g., 05/23/22, 05/24/22, 05/25/22). Table 2-4 is an example of an open price and close price panel dataset.

Table 2-4. Open price and close price panel dataset

Stock	Open price	Close price	Date
Apple	$137.79	$143.11	05/23/22
Apple	$140.81	$140.36	05/24/22
Apple	$138.43	$140.52	05/25/22
Google	$2,202.08	$2,333.33	05/23/22
Google	$2,127.55	$2,118.52	05/24/22
Google	$2,102.84	$2,116.79	05/25/22
IBM	$129.50	$131.17	05/23/22
IBM	$130.57	$133.80	05/24/22
IBM	$132.86	$134.39	05/25/22

Panel data has more than one variable or dimension and is therefore a multivariate dataset. The data can also be represented in three dimensions, as a three-dimensional matrix or tensor. Figure 2-4 illustrates the open price and close price cross-section data in a three-dimensional matrix where date is located on the x-axis (date), the open price and close price data elements are located on the y-axis (price), and the stock universe is located on the z-axis (stock). A specific price is located at the intersection of the date, price, and stock.

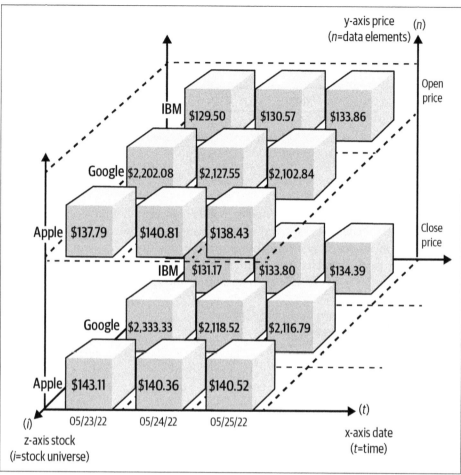

Figure 2-4. Close price and open price panel dataset, represented in three dimensions

Data Volumes

The term *volume*, as in a volume of data, is defined as the total count of all individual datums in the matrix. The term *data volume* is used to convey the shape of panel data in three dimensions, similar to a volume of raw materials used in manufacturing. Figure 2-5 illustrates that the total data volume for the close price and open price matrix is 18 price datums. When all the datums are visually represented close together, they form a cube.

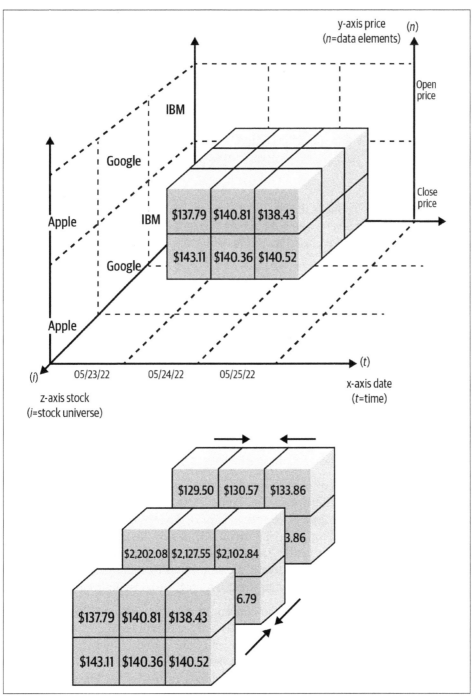

Figure 2-5. Close price and open price panel dataset, illustrated as a three-dimensional matrix volume

Think about the data volumes that are required to compute the market value of a portfolio, or the data volumes required to determine the correlation between two variables such as the stock price of a company and investor sentiment. For example, the portfolio market value calculation requires three data volumes:

- The volume of portfolio security positions with valid quantities on a specific date
- The volume of security instrument reference data that uniquely identifies the securities the position quantities reflect
- The volume of relevant prices (such as close price) for each security position on a specific date

The portfolio market value is then calculated by multiplying the position quantity by the close price. Generally, the portfolio market value is the sum of all individual security market values for all security positions within a specific portfolio, including any cash positions.

A data volume used in the financial industry is like a volume of raw material used in manufacturing (e.g., a pound of sand, a liter of water). Most of the data used in the financial services industry is panel data. A few examples of panel data as volumes of data include market data, fundamentals, securities and instruments, trades and transactions, portfolio positions, and performance measurement and attribution.

Of course, raw materials used in manufacturing differ from the data we use in the financial industry. The specifications for raw materials used in manufacturing have been optimized for purity, similarity, repeatability, and duplication to produce a consistent volume of material that uniformly conforms to precise specifications. For example, silica used for glass production must be chemically pure, contain more than 95% silicon dioxide, and have a grain size between 0.075 mm and 1.18 mm.

In the financial industry, however, a volume of data, unlike a volume of silica, is comprised of *unique* datums. Refer back to Figure 2-5 to see that there are 18 different and unique datums in the close price and open price data volume. The quality of each datum is individually and uniquely important. Generally, the *quality of every datum* used by a business function in the financial industry for critical operations such as conducting research, making investment decisions, trading securities, ensuring compliance, and reporting financial data to clients and regulators is important.

In the next section, we'll focus on the concept of data dimensions. This framework will help you understand the dimensions of data at the datum level, the quality validations in terms of tolerance or accuracy tests, and their applicability to different types of data. Applying dimensions to your data is the first step toward fully understanding the shape and quality of the data you are receiving from sources, the data you are about to use in your functional process, and the data you will be providing to another consumer or data processing application.

Data Dimensions and Attributes

Data has no mass or weight. Data contains no matter. Therefore, common physical measurement techniques do not apply. The size of data is often referred to in terms of the amount of recording media necessary to retain, preserve, and represent the digital binary code (the string of ones and zeroes) of data using computers and other electronic devices. How can data be measured if it has no physical form? How can the shape of data, which has no physical form, be understood and described beyond the size of media required to store it? Finally, how can the quality of the data be measured given the lack of physicality? We'll explore these questions in this section.

 Data dimensions is a practical framework applied to data that allows you to understand its shape and quality through specific measurements, as defined by a data consumer's data quality specification (DQS).

There are numerous examples of data dimensions from many thought leaders across many industries. The data dimensions in this book are intended to be used when measuring data quality relative to the DQS of consumers. As we'll see, "consumers" in this context could be a human, an application, or a business function. Assessing data quality is *the* most important task, after having acquired the data. The data dimensions presented in this section are quantitatively measurable. This is not an exercise to determine good data versus bad data. *Good* and *bad* are qualitative terms based in ethics and moral philosophy. Instead, this framework provides you with the tools to inspect every datum in a volume of data and validate whether the dimensions of the datum are within the data quality tolerance requirements of the consumer.

Figure 2-6 illustrates data dimensions and attributes associated with a single datum. *Data dimensions* are measurable characteristics of a specific datum (e.g., 7.45 or IBM) or instance of a data element (e.g., price or ticker). The dimensions of a specific datum are completeness, timeliness, accuracy, precision, conformity, congruence, collection, and cohesion.

Remember a datum is a single instance of a data element (e.g., price, country, name, issuer, quantity) that has multiple *attributes*, including definition, data type, security access policies, and so on. These attributes are often referred to as metadata that describe the characteristics of the data element.

The following sections discuss and define data attributes and data dimensions in more detail.

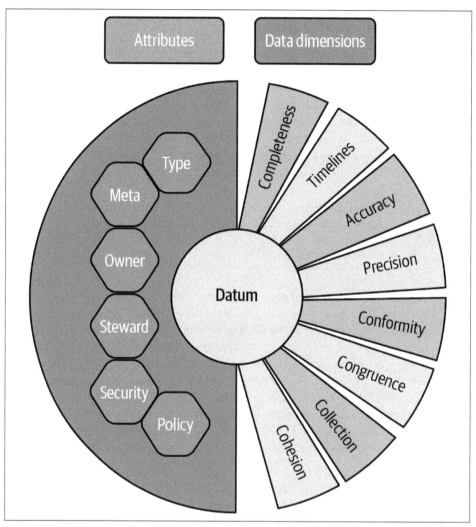

Figure 2-6. Data dimensions and attributes of a single datum

Data Attributes

Data attributes typically include the following:

Type
> May be numeric, character, or string, or a combination (alphanumeric).

Meta
> Any data (metadata) associated with the datum that describes or provides information about the data element (e.g., data definition, classification, origination).

Owner

The person or business function that has the highest level of subject matter expertise about the data. The data owner is typically the direct user and consumer of the data. They have authority over the data to make decisions about the data source, data quality, management methodology, integrity, and approved or unapproved uses of the data. Data owners typically define the DQS for the data to be considered "fit for purpose" for use by a business function or by the firm. Data owners typically do not manage the data. They generally do not have operational responsibility for the management and curation of the data.

Steward

This refers to data stewards, who typically make up an operational team that is devoted to, responsible for, and accountable for the management and curation of data. *Curation* includes the acquisition, definition and profiling, quality and integrity validation, data error remediation, metrics and score-carding, preservation, and dissemination of the data. Data stewards are responsible for delivering fit-for-purpose data, as defined by the data owner according to a DQS.

Security

This entails multiple considerations—from data masking and data access control to confidentiality, integrity, and physical storage. Data security and cybersecurity are two important considerations in data management.

Policy

This refers to guidelines and rules about the usage of the data. Data usage policies typically indicate the approved methods and business and technical processes for which data is permitted to be used. These policies may include guidelines that indicate which individuals or business functions are permitted to see and use the data, and whether the data can be stored, used to create derived data, or shared internally or externally (according to internal data control policies and vendor data license contracts).

Data Dimensions

Every datum has a completeness, or existence, dimension. This is the most basic test for any piece of data. If the datum does not exist, then you have nothing, and nothing has no other dimension. The other seven dimensions apply to data depending on its type and the context. Definitions of all eight data dimensions are as follows:

Completeness

This describes the existence or absence of data. You will need to determine whether the existence of the data is mandatory or optional.

Timeliness

This can refer to the timing, or date and time, associated with the data. It may also refer to the concept of fresh data versus stale data.

Accuracy

This refers to whether the data is valid and correct.

Precision

This often refers to the decimals of a number, but may also refer to a datum such as a code value that may be more or less precise than a comparative datum or a scale.

Conformity

This often refers to adhering to a specific format and, if relevant, can apply to any datum regardless of type.

Congruence

This refers to the similarity or difference in data over multiple time periods and generally applies to autocorrelated data.

Collection

This refers to a named group of data that together form a collection with all member datum present.

Cohesion

This refers to the relationship between one datum and some other datum. Generally, all data used in the financial industry relates to something, such as an issuer, stock, instrument, account, portfolio position, and so on.

Dimensions are intrinsic to data at the individual datum level. You can use the DQS framework, which we'll discuss in the next chapter, to determine the data quality tolerance test for each dimension. Data quality tolerance tests are applied to volumes of data across one or more dimensions to validate that the data satisfies the DQS of downstream consumers before the data is provided to the consumers.

 Generally, most of the dimensions apply to all data except the collection dimension. Collection refers to datum being a member of a collection. There are specific types of collections in the financial industry. Examples of collections of data include a portfolio of investment positions or the constituents of an index.

Table 2-5 summarizes the definitions and examples of each data dimension.

Table 2-5. Data dimension definitions and examples

Dimension	Definition	Examples
Completeness	Data exists and is not null	7
Timeliness	Staleness or freshness	Analyst recommendation: BUY, May 12, 2017
Accuracy	Valid, likelihood of correctness	Compare to authoritative source: 7 = 7 Triangulation—position quantity = 8, resulting from two transactions: buy 10 and sell 2
Precision	Decimals or being exact	7.00032
Conformity	Conforming to standards or rules	USA—ISO Alpha-2, USA—ISO Alpha-3
Congruence	Same or similar	7, 7.0, 7.03, 7.102, 7.004
Collection	All required applicable datum components exist	Portfolio containing positions or an index containing constituents
Cohesion	Relationship alignment to other data	Position: SEDOL = Security: SEDOL

Summary

Datasets are like volumes of raw materials used in manufacturing. Data volumes usually contain many individual datum values that have shape and dimensions. Typically, multiple data volumes are required to satisfy an analytical use case in financial services. Data quality, integrity, and cohesion are the most important factors that determine the viability of a data volume. The quality, consistency, and cohesion of the data volume should be analyzed, assessed, measured, understood, validated, and certified according to a DQS before it is used. In the next chapter, you will learn how to use the DQS framework to define data quality tolerances for dimensions at the datum level.

CHAPTER 3

Data Quality Specifications

This chapter defines *valid* (within tolerance), *suspect* (approaching tolerance bounds), and *invalid* (out of tolerance) conditions, relative to the applicable data dimensions at the datum level. These conditions reflect the data quality specifications (DQS) of the downstream consumer. This chapter will detail an approach to data validation that ensures alignment with the DQS of a consumer.

Manufacturing Controls

Recall from Chapter 1 that *manufacturing* refers to the production of products using labor, machines, tools, chemical and biological processing, or formulation. *Industrial manufacturing* is the transformation of raw materials into finished products at scale. The manufacturing processes in the production pipeline are controlled using *quality control and assurance plans and specifications.*

Just like manufacturing uses control specifications, the financial industry uses precise DQS to engineer data quality validations, to control data quality, and to identify data anomalies. Data quality is assessed *before* the data is provisioned to downstream processes, applications, or consumers. DQS will differ depending on the consumer use cases. Pre-use data validations prevent data that does not satisfy DQS from polluting the downstream data ecosystem. Data quality validations use anomaly and outlier detection techniques that identify items, events, patterns, and observations that do not conform to specifications, tolerances, and expected patterns, or that lack relationship to other items in a dataset.

DQS Overview

Data quality specifications (DQS) define the data tolerance requirements of the downstream consumer and the expectations about the shape and quality of the data that will be received and used. The tolerance requirements are applied to select data dimensions for each datum of a data element. These tolerances are typically embedded in a data quality validation application or platform, and they represent data quality rules. The rules generate data quality metrics about datum values, which can then be compared to the tolerances specified for a specific data element. The business readiness, fit-for-purpose, and business impact classifications are also based on the metrics generated from analyzing the data relative to the data quality validation rules.

The DQS are used to align and embed data quality validations and data controls in the data management and distribution infrastructure. The DQS framework is used to document data elements and define the data quality tolerances for data volumes used by each target application or consumer. DQS documentation requirements include defining the DQS for each data element and the datum validation metrics (in the form of measurable tolerances).

The DQS may assign a business impact level that refers to the negative impact on the consumer or application in the event of failed data quality validations. Such failures occur when the tolerance checks for one or more specified datum indicate the data quality measurements exceed the quality tolerances. Aside from negative impact, the DQS may specify the following business impact levels that can be used to prioritize the importance of the data and the data remediation response:

H = High impact
> The impact to the consumer or application is *high* and the process to use the data is in a failure state. This level of business impact means an immediate response and data remediation are typically required.

M = Medium impact
> The impact to the consumer or application is *medium* and the process to use the data is still operational. However, the consumer or application is impaired in some way and is unable to fully operate with the data. This level of business impact means triage and data remediation. Reprocessing the data is typically required, but the issue and impact are not considered critical.

L = Low impact
> The impact to the consumer or application is *low* and the process to use the data is still operational. The consumer or application impairment is minor and is still able to operate with or without the data. This level of business impact may mean triage, data remediation, and reprocessing the data (though, given the low business impact, reprocessing may be deemed not necessary).

Data Quality Tolerances

Data quality tolerances are specified in the DQS for each data element at the data element or data collection level. Refer back to Figure 2-6, which illustrates data dimensions and attributes associated with the data.

The data quality tolerance codes for data dimensions (e.g., completeness, timeliness, accuracy, precision) are as follows:

M = Mandatory
  Means the datum is required to exist

O = Optional
  Means the datum may or may not exist

V = Valid/within tolerance
  Means the evaluation of the datum is within valid tolerance

S = Suspect/approaching out of tolerance
  Means the evaluation of the datum is *between* valid tolerance and invalid/out of tolerance

IV = Invalid/out of tolerance
  Means the evaluation of the datum is outside both valid and suspect tolerances

All tolerances are based on the data quality expectations of the consumer or application.

Completeness

You may recall from Chapter 2 that *completeness* is the data dimension that reflects the existence or absence of data. You need to determine whether the existence of the data is mandatory or optional. Every datum has a completeness or existence dimension. This is the most basic test for any piece of data. If the datum does not exist, then you have nothing. A datum without any value contains nothing and is empty—it may be represented by an empty string or null. The value zero does not mean an empty datum. Likewise, a string of blank spaces is not an empty datum. If a datum has no data, then you have nothing. Nothing has no dimensions and cannot be measured. However, you can count the number of empty strings or nulls.

These codes are used to specify the data quality tolerance for the completeness dimension at the datum level:

M = Mandatory
> Means there should be no empty strings or nulls; the datum *must* exist

O = Optional
> Means there may be empty strings or nulls; the datum may or may not exist, but it is *not mandatory* to exist

V = Valid/within tolerance
> Means the data exists

S = Suspect
> Means the data may or may not exist, but the existence of the data is not mandatory

IV = Invalid/out of tolerance
> Means the data does not exist and the existence of the data is mandatory

A simple example of the DQS is to calculate the market value of a portfolio position. Here, the position quantity is multiplied by close price. The close price completeness is mandatory (M), thus the datum must exist. Close price tolerance is valid (V) if the data exists and invalid (IV) if the data is empty. The business impact is high if any of the prices are empty.

Tolerances for completeness can be expressed in shorthand as follows:

> *data element: data dimension = mandatory or optional, valid, or invalid condition, business impact*

In our simple example, the completeness validation metric expressed in shorthand is as follows:

close price: completeness = M, IV ≥ 1, H

The shorthand notation means the validation check for the completeness dimension of the close price data element is mandatory and the data must exist. If the count of missing close price data is equal to or greater than one, then the missing datum is invalid, and the business impact is high. The shorthand notation is useful when capturing the data quality validation requirement and expressing the requirement in condensed form for encoding into data quality validation checks.

Example

The DQS for generating a histogram of available prices from a data vendor for a universe of stocks on a single day may or may not include a price for all the stocks in the universe. The consumer indicates that, in order for the data volume to be useful, prices must exist for at least 60% of the stocks in the universe. If there are empty prices for more than 40% of the stocks in the universe, then the data volume is not useful, and the business impact is high. If there are empty prices for 20% to 40% of the stocks in the universe, then the data volume may be useful, but the consumer is suspicious of the viability of the data and the business impact is medium.

The available prices completeness validation check is optional (O) and the datum may or may not exist. Available prices tolerances are valid (V) if the volume of prices exists for greater than 80% of the stock universe, suspect (S) if the volume of empty prices is between 20% and 40% of the stocks in the universe, and invalid (IV) if the volume of empty prices is greater than 40% of the stocks in the universe. The completeness validation metric is expressed as follows:

available prices: completeness = O, V ≥ 80%, S ≥ 60% and < 80%, M, IV < 60%, H

Timeliness

Timeliness is the term used to describe the temporality dimension of the data relative to an expectation about the timing of the data, as defined in the DQS of the consumer. Most of the data used in the financial industry is time series data and includes date, time, timestamps, or date-time data elements. This means the data is a set of individual data points in a sequence recorded at successive, evenly spaced intervals of time. A datum from 10 years ago may be considered valid for a historical data analysis, but the same datum may be considered invalid if the DQS for a consumer or application indicate only data that has been recently recorded (e.g., in the past week) is considered valid.

These codes are used to specify the data quality tolerance for the timeliness dimension, at the datum level:

V = Valid/within tolerance
> Means a) the date, time, or date-time datum is within the valid reference temporal *range* or b) a *specific* date, time, or date-time matches the valid reference temporality.

S = Suspect
> Means if the DQS include the concept of approaching out of tolerance, but not exceeding the invalid tolerance, then the suspect tolerance can be used. Suspect means the date, time, or date-time datum is *between* the valid tolerance and the invalid tolerance reference temporal ranges. The suspect tolerance does not apply to DQS for *specific* dates, times or date-times.

IV = Invalid/out of tolerance
> Means a) the date, time, or date-time datum is outside the valid reference temporal *range* and, if applicable, outside the suspect tolerance range or b) a *specific* date, time, or date-time does not match the valid reference temporality.

Example

The DQS for a volume of analyst data used to create consensus estimates for the upcoming quarter would include a validation for the timeliness dimension. The DQS in this example require the date of the estimate to be within the past three months from today. The DQS also indicate that analyst estimates are suspect if their date is greater than two months old but less than three months old. Finally, analyst estimates with dates greater than three months old are not useful. This example uses 06/13/2022 as today and 30 as the number of days in a month.

The timeliness validation metric for analyst estimates is valid (V) if the date of the estimate is between 06/13/2022 and a historical date 60 days prior to today (04/14/2022), suspect (S) if the date of the estimate is between 04/13/2022 and 03/14/2022 (then the business impact is low), and invalid (IV) if the date of the estimate is less than 03/14/2022 (then the business impact is low). The timeliness validation metric is expressed as follows:

> *analyst estimate date: timeliness = O, V ≤ 60 days, 60 days > S ≤ 90 days, L, IV > 90 days, L*

The timeliness validation metric may be applied to any time series data volume where the date, time, or date-time of the datum must match a specific date, time, or date-time or must be within a temporal range that is required per the DQS of a consumer. Market data, fundamentals, trades, transactions, cash flows, corporate actions, analyst estimates, portfolio holdings, and performance returns are all examples of *temporal panel data volumes*. A temporal panel data volume is a time series cross-section with more than one data element. The temporal panel data volume is the most complex time series.

Accuracy

Accuracy refers to, of course, how correct something is. The accuracy data dimension is typically unique to the datum. Generally, you can compare the datum to an authoritative data source known to be correct. This is a direct data validation check. Alternatively, you can use data triangulation, which is an indirect validation technique. *Data triangulation* refers to the use of data from alternate data sources, data volumes, calculations, or alternate time periods relative to the datum under inspection. The triangulation technique does not directly confirm the accuracy of the datum under inspection. However, the inspection of other data, relative to the datum under inspection, provides an indirect validation check.

To summarize, the accuracy of the datum can be validated using:

Authoritative source comparison
    Direct accuracy validation using cross-reference comparison to authoritative data from a verified data source or comparison to control data

Data triangulation
    Indirect accuracy validation using computations, calculations, and cross-footing, or indirectly validated using comparison to other related data

These codes are used to specify the data quality tolerance for the accuracy dimension, at the datum level:

V = Valid/within tolerance
    Means accuracy is directly confirmed via authoritative source comparison and the data is correct, or means the data is *likely* accurate using indirect triangulation

S = Suspect
    Means unable to verify accuracy due to the lack of a) the authoritative source data or b) the other data intended for use in triangulation is not available or usable

IV = Invalid/out of tolerance
    Means accuracy is directly confirmed via authoritative source comparison and the data is incorrect, or means the data is *likely* incorrect using indirect triangulation

The following symbols are used to specify the data relationship in the accuracy validation:

+

The data elements are used together in the data validation.

=

The data elements used for authoritative comparison are equivalent.

≠

The data elements used for authoritative comparison are not equivalent.

~

The data elements used for triangulation have a valid relationship or equivalency.

!~

The data elements used for triangulation do not have a valid relationship or equivalency.

Authoritative data source

Authoritative data source comparison is a robust way to validate the accuracy dimension of a datum by comparing the datum to a data source known to be correct. The comparison of position quantities in a data volume received as a data file and the position quantities in the source accounting system is an example of authoritative source comparison. This is a technique often used by operations teams to confirm whether the portfolio holdings quantities in a local data volume match the values in the source accounting system. You can use authoritative datasets, including standardized country codes, currency codes, and industry classification codes, from authoritative sources for direct comparison to data received from data aggregator vendors.

Example

An example of an authoritative data source is a data volume of verified ticker symbols that are registered and traded on a securities exchange—for example, National Association of Securities Dealers Automated Quotations (NASDAQ), New York Stock Exchange (NYSE), Tokyo Stock Exchange (TSE), or Deutsche Börse Group. The ticker symbol and exchange are used to determine the trading venue for a particular security. The consumer of this data indicates that if the ticker symbol is not a valid ticker for an exchange, the data is incorrect and not usable, and the impact is high. The ticker symbol and exchange in this dataset can be compared against ticker symbol and exchange data from another data source to verify the ticker symbol and exchange relationship is correct. The accuracy validation metric is expressed as follows:

ticker symbol: accuracy—authoritative = V, ticker symbol + exchange = ticker symbol + exchange, IV, ticker symbol + exchange ≠ ticker symbol + exchange, H

Most of the industry and market data used in financial services is sourced from data vendors that aggregate and consolidate data from many authoritative sources. Therefore, it is generally impractical to confirm the accuracy of large and diverse data volumes (e.g., market data, fundamentals, analyst estimates) using authoritative data source comparison. The industry generally relies on its experience with the vendors' strengths and expertise to gather, ingest, cleanse, harmonize, and distribute large, high-quality data volumes they sell as data products to their clients. But, mistakes can be made.

Triangulation

Triangulation refers to the use of other data elements, calculations, and comparisons as an indirect validation check of the accuracy of a datum. For example, an accounting service company provides you with a data file containing portfolio holdings records and one additional record that includes the market value of the portfolio. The summation of the market value of the portfolio holdings records should equal the market value provided by the accounting service. In this example, the summation of the portfolio holdings market value equals $430,000 and the market value record indicates the portfolio market value is $395,000. Here, we are using the summation of the portfolio holdings market values compared to the stated market value as an indirect accuracy validation. The accuracy validation metric is expressed as follows:

market value: accuracy—triangulation = V, Σ holdings market value = market value, IV, Σ holdings market value ≠ market value, H

Example

The use of ticker, local currency, and price can be used as a triangulation validation check. For example, the Apple Inc. ticker symbol on the NASDAQ stock exchange is AAPL. Let's say the share price is $131.56 in local currency (USD). Apple stock data, along with many other securities, is in a financial securities data volume. The consumer of this data expects the security record to contain the ticker symbol and the current price and local currency. If the price is incorrect, then the data cannot be used, and the business impact is high.

The data in this data volume contains the Apple security record, and the ticker symbol is APC with a price of $126.06 in USD. You can use triangulation to validate the currency of the price relative to the ticker symbol and local currency. The ticker symbol APC is the symbol for Apple Inc. on the Frankfurt securities exchange—those securities trade in euros, not USD. Therefore, the triangulation validation uses the APC and the USD price to indirectly validate either the ticker symbol, the price, the local currency, or a combination of the datum used here is incorrect. The ticker symbol APC in this data volume should have a price of €126.06 in local currency (euros). The accuracy validation metric is expressed as follows:

price: accuracy—triangulation = V, ticker symbol ~ price + local currency, IV, ticker symbol !~ price + local currency, H

The accuracy dimension, as previously stated, is unique to the datum under inspection and often requires specialized authoritative source comparison or customizing the triangulation validation check with the relevant alternative data to create an indirect accuracy validation.

 Authoritative source comparison is a very robust, direct data accuracy validation technique. Triangulation can be helpful and useful to indicate the *likelihood* of data alignment or misalignment, but due to the indirect nature of the validation logic and use of other related data that may also be incorrect, it is often a poor indicator to specifically validate accuracy and identify the incorrect datum.

Precision

The term *precision* commonly refers to the number of digits in a number, and *scale* refers to the number of digits to the right of the decimal point in a number. The precision data dimension in this framework refers to the scale of the number that conveys how precise it is. For example, the number 389.2 has one digit to the right of the decimal versus the number 389.24846 that has five digits to the right of the decimal. The number 389.24846 is more precise than the number 389.2. While precision is extremely important in mathematical computation, it is especially important when using numbers in calculations in the financial industry.

These codes are used to specify the data quality tolerance for the precision dimension, at the datum level:

V = Valid/within tolerance
    Means the datum has the required scale or decimals

S = Suspect
    Means the datum has a scale or the number of decimals that is *between* the valid tolerance and the invalid tolerance

IV = Invalid/out of tolerance
    Means the datum does not have the required scale or decimals

Example: Exchange rate

Exchanging one currency for another is a simple example of how the precision can yield different results. Exchange rates in financial calculations are typically expressed with four and as many as six decimals. This is the generally accepted exchange cross rate precision in the financial industry. Exchanging $200,000 (USD) for euros using cross rates 1.05 and 1.059047 yields €190,476.19 and €188,849.03, respectively, with a difference of $1,627.16. The precision dimension in the DQS is especially important to consumers and applications that require very precise numeric data for calculations. The use of imprecise rates of return, basis point differences, and valuations in transactions and calculations can lead to highly inaccurate data. When it comes to the numbers in the financial industry, precision is one of the most important dimensions—it can have tremendous negative impact on a financial firm, including loss of assets, loss of clients, regulatory fines, and financial penalties. The DQS for the precision validation metric for this example is valid (V) if the number has six decimals, and invalid (IV) if the number has less than six decimals. The business impact is high. The precision validation metric is expressed as follows:

cross rate: precision—decimal = V = 6, IV < 6, H

Example: Market values

Prices used to calculate market values may be more or less precise based on the number of decimals. For example, the market value of an account holding one hundred shares of a single equity security is calculated using a price of $23.45 and $23.454890 yields $2,345.00 and $2,345.489, respectively. While the difference is only $0.489 cents, this error compounds with successive calculations using the less precise number. If the price used was less precise and only included four decimals, such as $23.4548, then the market value is $2,345.48. The example indicates four decimals is potentially acceptable to the consumer, but may be considered suspicious. The DQS for the precision validation metric for this example indicate valid (V) if the number has five or six decimals, suspect (S) if the number has four decimals (the business impact is medium), and invalid (IV) if the number has three or less decimals (the business impact is high). The precision validation metric is expressed as follows:

prices: precision—decimal = V ≥ 5, S = 4, M, IV ≤ 3, H

Precision and precision misalignment are often overlooked due to the complexities of storing and processing numbers using data structures, such as data typed files (e.g., Apache Parquet), database data typed columns (e.g., Microsoft Structured Query Language (SQL) Server, Oracle, Snowflake) and data type objects in programming languages (e.g., Python, R). You need to ensure the precision required in the DQS for a consumer or application is consistent throughout the data structures and data processing applications. You also need to be vigilant about any intentional or unintentional rounding or truncation operations used within numeric calculations.

Conformity

The *conformity* dimension relates to whether a data element conforms to a specific data standard or a specific format (e.g., alpha, alphanumeric, date, or numeric). There are numerous examples of conformity, including date, time, ISO country codes, ISO currency codes, specialized classification code sets, and so on.

These codes are used to specify the data quality tolerance for the conformity dimension, at the datum level:

V = Valid/within tolerance
　　Means the data conforms to the required format or standard

IV = Invalid/out of tolerance
　　Means the data does not conform to the required format or standard

Example

Consider the example of industry classifications as a grouping mechanism in a client report. The DQS require the industry classifications of issuers of securities be assigned to the security positions in a portfolio holdings data volume. The MSCI/S&P Global Industry Classification Standard (GICS®) data includes code values (e.g., the energy industry group GICS code is 1010). The full set of GICS classification codes from the data vendor can be used as the reference dataset for comparing the GICS code values in the portfolio positions data volume. This comparison validates whether the GICS code in a data volume matches a GICS code in the reference dataset.

The DQS for using GICS as a grouping category of portfolio holdings in a client report require all portfolio positions to have an assigned GICS code. The conformity validation metric is expressed as follows:

　　GICS code: conformity = V, = format, IV, ≠ format, H

Generally, the metric is binary and means a datum either does or does not conform to the required DQS format or standard. This example confirms the GICS codes in the portfolio holdings data volume are valid and conform to the GICS standard; however, it doesn't mean the GICS code assigned to that position in the holdings data volume is the correct code. You will also need an accuracy validation check, using authoritative source comparison, to determine whether the correct code is assigned to a specific issuer. In addition, you will need a completeness validation check to determine if there are any missing GICS codes, since the DQS require all security positions in the portfolio holdings data volume to have an assigned GICS code.

ISO country codes are a good example of a simple format requirement. ISO country codes comprise either two or three characters that define the country code. If the DQS for the country code data element in a data volume require the ISO country code to conform to the two-character format, then the conformity validation can be applied to the datum to verify whether it is two characters. Often, when using the conformity validation, you can also include an accuracy validation that will validate both that the code is the proper length and that the code is a valid country code.

The conformity validation can be applied to any data when DQS indicate there is a required format. For example, the conformity validation can be applied to dates to validate the date format. There are many different date formats—MM/DD/YYYY, MM/DD/YY, DD/MM/YY, and so on.

Congruence

The *congruence* dimension refers to the similarity of a specific datum to other observations of the data element (e.g., close price, open price, analyst estimate, portfolio return, account holdings market value) for a specific data entity (e.g., stock, issuer, analyst, account, account position) over multiple time intervals. As we've discussed, most of the data used in financial services is time series data and for a specific data element. Most of the time series data is linearly correlated over time. For example, an equity stock price today can be compared to the price of the same stock from prior time periods. The methodology of generating the price on a stock trading exchange is consistent from one day to the next; therefore, you can compare the stock price from today to the stock price from yesterday, or to previous historical instances of the prices. The stock price data is autocorrelated data.

You can apply congruence validations to alpha and alphanumeric data as well. For example, let's say the country of domicile for an issuer has consistently been the United States for the past 10 years. The issuer data volume from a data vendor indicates the country of domicile changed from the United States to the United Kingdom. The change in the country of domicile may be valid due to the company moving its corporate headquarters and domicile from one country to another, but the change could also be invalid due to a vendor error.

Similarly, if the stock price today is significantly higher or lower, relative to a tolerance range, than the historical stock prices for the same stock, then the stock price today is an outlier. The stock price may be a valid price, or it may be invalid due to an error. Congruence validation checks do not validate the accuracy of a datum. Instead, congruence checks provide quantitative measurement of the similarity, or congruence, of the datum compared to historical observations of the same data element within tolerances. Data is considered highly congruent when the similarity between a specific datum and historical values of the same data element is within a valid tolerance range.

You can use congruence checks to validate data is within valid tolerance ranges and to identify anomalies and outliers that are outside of valid and suspect tolerance ranges. Here are the various types of congruence validation checks:

Comparison to prior value
Comparison of a numeric, alpha, or alphanumeric datum to the most recent prior historical instance of the datum

Comparison to average
Comparison of a numeric datum to the statistical average of the historical instances of the datum

Comparison to standard deviation and z-score
Comparison of the datum to the calculated standard deviation and z-score of the historical datum

These validation checks are simple statistical calculations or datum value comparisons. You are encouraged to develop your own congruence validation checks using more sophisticated logic that may be more applicable for identifying anomalies in your data.

These codes are used to specify the data quality tolerance for the congruence dimension, at the datum level:

V = Valid/within tolerance
Means the metric generated from applying the congruence validation methodology to the datum is within the valid tolerance

S = Suspect
Means the metric generated from applying the congruence validation methodology to the datum is between the valid tolerance and the invalid tolerance

IV = Invalid/out of tolerance
Means the metric generated from applying the congruence validation methodology to the datum is outside the valid tolerance

Prior value comparison

Prior value comparison means comparing the value of a datum with the most recent prior historical value of the same datum. The comparison of the Apple stock close price today with the Apple stock close price from yesterday is an example of prior value comparison for the Apple stock data entity. Similarly, an issuer country of domicile today can be compared with the country of domicile for the same issuer data entity from yesterday.

The prior value comparison metric for alpha and alphanumeric data is generated by comparing the data value from one point in time to the data value of the same data element from the immediately preceding point in time. String matching techniques are typically used for prior value comparison using alpha and alphanumeric data. For example, the three-character ISO country code USA is used to designate the country of domicile datum value in an issuer data volume. The DQS for the use of the country of domicile codes in determining whether a stock can be bought, held, or sold based on regulatory country sanctions indicate that any change from the approved countries from the prior period be identified and the stock blocked from trading. The compliance department requires the country code remain consistent from one day to the next and only stocks from approved countries can be traded. If a stock is traded from an issuer from a sanctioned country, then the firm will incur financial penalties and regulatory fines, and the business impact is high.

You can use the prior value comparison check to validate whether the country of domicile datum for an issuer today is consistent with the country of domicile for the same issuer from yesterday, or the nearest historical point in time prior to today. In this example, if the country code today is USA and the country code from yesterday is USA, then they match. The country of domicile datum value for this issuer is congruent based on prior value comparison. If the country today is IRN (Iran), but the country code from yesterday is USA, then they do not match and the country of domicile datum value for this issuer is incongruent based on prior value comparison. The prior value comparison congruence validation metric is expressed as follows:

country of domicile: prior value congruence = V, = match, IV, ≠ match, H

The prior value comparison metric for a numeric data element is generated by calculating the percentage difference between the numeric value for a data element from one point in time and the numeric value for the same data element from the immediately preceding point in time. For example, the difference between the two numbers is expressed as a percentage. The comparison of the Apple stock close price today of $138.16 with the Apple stock close price from yesterday of $136.44 is an example of prior value comparison of the close price for the Apple stock data entity.

Example

A data volume that contains three years of stock ticker symbols and close prices with a corresponding date for a universe of one thousand issuers is intended to be used to analyze the daily change in the close price for a stock relative to positive or negative news sentiment about the issuer of the stock. The DQS for the use of the stock price data volume indicate that any close price datum with a difference from one day versus the prior day that is less than 10% is considered valid and the close price datum in the time series for a given data entity is useful. If the close price datum difference from one day versus the prior day is 10% or greater (up to and including 20%), then the close price datum for that data entity for that date is considered suspect and the close price time series data may or may not be useful but is considered suspicious (the business impact is low). If the close price datum difference from one day versus the prior day is greater than 20%, then the close price datum for that data entity for that date is considered invalid, the close price time series data is not useful, and the business impact is medium.

The prior value comparison congruence validation metric is expressed as follows:

close price: prior value congruence = V %lt; 10%, S ≥ 10% and ≤ 20%, L, IV > 20%, H

Table 3-1 illustrates the prior value calculation and resulting congruence validation metric based on the DQS. These are the calculation formulas used to generate the prior value comparison results for a specific date:

Prior value absolute difference = (close price for a specific date – close price for the prior date)

Prior value percent difference = (prior value absolute difference)/((close price for a specific date + close price for the prior date) / 2) × 100

Table 3-1. Prior value congruence comparison

Date	Stock ticker	Close price	Prior value absolute difference	Prior value percent difference	Congruence validation metric
06/23/22	AAPL	$158.32	$26.76	18.46%	Suspect
06/22/22	AAPL	$131.56	$1.34	1.02%	Valid
06/21/22	AAPL	$130.22	$0.33	0.25%	Valid
06/17/22	AAPL	$129.89	$1,170.37	163.67%	Invalid
06/16/22	AAPL	$1,300.26	$1,170.16	163.61%	Invalid
06/15/22	AAPL	$130.10	$1.42	1.08%	Valid
06/14/22	AAPL	$131.52	N/A	N/A	N/A

The prior value comparison can be useful for detecting outliers based on tolerances for percentage differences between datum values in a time series data volume. Generally, this congruence check is used to identify large differences that most likely indicate spurious data. If the tolerances for the percentage differences are very narrow, this validation check will likely produce many false positive data metrics indicating data that is suspect or invalid when it is in fact valid. If the tolerances are set too wide, this validation check will not identify potentially invalid data. This congruence check is commonly used with wide tolerances such that data that exceeds the valid and suspect tolerances is generally recognized as invalid, based on experience with the data. If the nature of the data indicates that each datum should always or mostly be very similar in value, then more narrow tolerances can be used.

Comparison to average

Comparison to the average or mean is applied only to numeric data and means comparing the value of a datum with the average of the historical values of the same data element. The comparison of the Apple stock close price today with the average Apple stock close price from the past year is an example of the comparison to average congruence check for the Apple stock data entity. The comparison of the Apple stock close price today of $138.16 with the average of Apple stock close prices from prior dates of $134.55 is an example of comparison to average of the close price for the Apple stock data entity.

Example

A data volume that contains three years of stock ticker symbols and close prices with a corresponding date for a universe of one thousand issuers is intended to be used to analyze the daily change in the close price for a stock relative to positive or negative news sentiment about the issuer of the stock. The DQS for the use of the stock price data volume indicate any close price difference from the average of all other historical close price data for the same data entity that is less than 2% is considered valid and the close price datum in the time series for a given data entity is useful. If the close price difference from the average close price is 2% or greater (up to and including 3%), then the close price datum for that data entity for that date is considered suspect, and the close price time series data may or may not be useful but is considered suspicious and the business impact is low. If the close price difference from the average close price is greater than 3%, then the close price datum for that data entity for that date is considered invalid, and the close price time series data is not useful; the business impact is medium. The comparison to average congruence validation metric is expressed as follows:

close price: average congruence = V < 2%, S ≥ 2% and ≤ 3%, L, IV > 3%, H

Table 3-2 illustrates the calculation of the average close price and resulting congruence validation metric based on the DQS. The calculation of the mathematical average, or mean, close price is the sum of all close prices divided by the number of close prices.

Table 3-2. Comparison to average congruence

Date	Stock ticker	Close price	Average close price	Absolute difference	Comparison to average percent difference	Congruence validation metric
06/23/22	AAPL	$158.32	$134.55	$23.77	4.058%	Invalid
06/22/22	AAPL	$131.56	$134.55	$2.99	0.562%	Valid
06/21/22	AAPL	$130.22	$134.55	$4.33	0.818%	Valid
06/17/22	AAPL	$129.89	$134.55	$4.66	0.882%	Valid
06/16/22	AAPL	$130.26	$134.55	$4.29	0.811%	Valid
06/15/22	AAPL	$130.10	$134.55	$4.45	0.841%	Valid
06/14/22	AAPL	$131.52	$134.55	$3.03	0.570%	Valid

The comparison to average or mean can be useful for detecting outliers based on tolerances for percentage differences between a specific datum and the average or mean of the same data element datum in a time series data volume. Generally, this congruence check is used to identify differences that most likely indicate spurious data where you expect small fluctuations in the datum values. For example, corporations do issue new shares of stock; however, this is a relatively infrequent event. Therefore, the number of outstanding stock shares from a company tends to remain constant over lengthy periods of time. Exchange rates are another example of financial data that does fluctuate, but generally the fluctuations are small.

The comparison to average check can also be useful for detecting percentage differences, but if the tolerances for the percentage differences are very narrow, this validation check will likely produce many false positive data metrics indicating data that is suspect or invalid when it is in fact valid. If the tolerances are set too wide, this validation check will not identify potentially invalid data. This congruence check is commonly used with wide tolerances, such that data that exceeds the valid and suspect tolerances is generally recognized as invalid, based on experience with the data. If the nature of the data indicates the datum values should always or mostly be very similar, thus close to the average of the data, then more narrow tolerances can be used. The average or mean is a measure of central tendency and is always affected by outliers. Therefore, the use of the mean in the comparison to average congruence check works best if the historical data used to calculate the average has been previously validated.

Comparison to standard deviation and z-score

Standard deviation and z-score measurements are only applied to numeric data. The z-score is a measurement that indicates a datum value's relationship to the average or mean of a set of values for the same data element for the same data entity within a date range. The z-score is expressed in terms of standard deviations from the mean. This validation check is generally more useful for identifying suspect or invalid data than prior value comparison or comparison to the average because the standard deviation and z-score calculations use a time range to constrain the sample set of data.

Market volatility is a term used to describe exceptional price movements in stocks and illustrates the use of z-score. If you use the comparison to average check and compare the most recent price with the average of all prices of a specific stock over multiple years, the comparison is likely to demonstrate that the stock price today is very different than the average of all the stock prices. Here's one way to think about this: a recent datum value, such as a stock price in time relative to all current market conditions, is more comparable to other recent stock prices for the same stock versus comparing a recent stock price to one from many years ago. The z-score validation check includes a time range boundary that is used to constrain the datum values in the calculation. This means you can compare the z-score of a recent datum value with the z-score of other recent datum values in a specific time range. You can use standard deviation tolerances with the z-score to generate the congruence metric and determine if a datum is within the valid, suspect, or invalid tolerances.

Example

The close prices from yesterday for a universe of one thousand issuers are intended to be used to calculate the market value of a portfolio for yesterday. You have the close prices from yesterday and you have a data volume that contains five years of stock ticker symbols and close prices for the issuer universe. The DQS for the use of the stock close prices indicate any most recent close price datum for a data entity be two or less z-score standard deviations from the mean in a historical close price sample period of five business days. Close prices that are two or less z-score standard deviations from the mean are considered valid, and the close price data is valid and useful. If the close price is greater than two (up to four) z-score standard deviations from the mean, then the close price datum for that data entity for that date is considered suspect, and the close price datum may or may not be useful but is considered suspicious; the business impact is high. If the close price is greater than four or more z-score standard deviations from the mean, then the close price datum for that data entity for that date is considered invalid, and the close price datum is not useful; the business impact is high.

The z-score congruence validation metric includes the date range and is expressed as follows:

close price: z-score congruence = range 5 business days, V ≤ 2, S > 2 and < 4, H, IV ≥ 4, H

Table 3-3 illustrates the calculation of the average close price, standard deviation, z-score, and resulting congruence validation metric based on the DQS.

These are the calculation formulas used to generate the standard deviation and z-score results for this example:

Arithmetic average or mean
> The calculation of the mathematical average or mean close price for the datum values from the prior five business days for the purpose of generating the z-score is the sum of the close prices for the prior five business days divided by five.

Z-score
> The calculation of the z-score is the close price under inspection minus the mean close price of the prior five business days divided by the standard deviation of the close prices of the prior five business days.

Table 3-3. Standard deviation and z-score congruence

Date	Stock ticker	Close price	Average close price for prior 5 business days	Close price – average close price for prior 5 business days	Standard deviation of close prices for prior 5 business days	Absolute z-score	Congruence validation metric
06/23/22	AAPL	$158.32	$130.41	$27.91	0.660969	42.23	Invalid
06/22/22	AAPL	$131.56	$130.40	$1.16	0.643522	1.8	Valid
06/21/22	AAPL	$130.22	$136.80	$- 6.58	14.238948	0.46	Valid
06/17/22	AAPL	$129.89	$136.58	$- 6.69	14.381631	0.47	Valid
06/16/22	AAPL	$130.26	$136.61	$- 6.35	14.364215	0.44	Valid
06/15/22	AAPL	$130.10	$136.82	$- 6.72	14.252415	0.47	Valid
06/14/22	AAPL	$131.52	$136.72	$- 5.20	14.304605	0.36	Valid
06/10/22	AAPL	$162.25	$129.92	$32.33	1.317353	24.54	Invalid
06/09/22	AAPL	$128.78	$129.93	$- 1.15	1.304607	0.88	Valid
06/08/22	AAPL	$130.42	N/A	N/A	N/A	N/A	N/A
06/07/22	AAPL	$131.15	N/A	N/A	N/A	N/A	N/A
06/06/22	AAPL	$130.98	N/A	N/A	N/A	N/A	N/A
06/03/22	AAPL	$128.26	N/A	N/A	N/A	N/A	N/A
06/02/22	AAPL	$128.84	N/A	N/A	N/A	N/A	N/A

The standard deviation and z-score congruence check tends to be more useful than prior value comparison and comparison to average for detecting outliers. The prior value comparison check only demonstrates the difference between two numbers. The comparison to average check also only demonstrates the difference between two numbers and the arithmetic average or mean calculation that is always affected by the trending differences in historical datum values, as well as outliers. Additionally, since most of the time series data in the financial industry tends to have long histories of datum values, the datum values from one time period relative to market and economic conditions at that time tend to be quite different than those from a more distant period in time, relative to the market and economic conditions at that time.

The standard deviation and z-score check uses a date range as a windowing function to localize the calculation of the average or mean of datum values in the time series that are close to the datum value under inspection. Therefore, the use of standard deviation and z-score tends to be a more *precise* data validation check for identifying spurious data.

Collection

The collection data dimension refers to special data volumes used in the financial industry. By definition, a *collection* refers to a group or specific set of things. A portfolio of holdings and an index of constituents are two commonly recognized data collections. All portfolio holdings for a given portfolio must exist to have a valid portfolio collection. Likewise, all constituents for a given index must exist to have a valid index. For example, the S&P 500 Index is a stock market index containing fice hundred large companies listed on exchanges in the United States. You must have all five hundred constituent data records for the S&P 500 index to be considered a valid data collection. If even only one constituent of the index is missing or cannot be identified, then you do not have a valid index collection. The same logic applies to portfolios of holdings. If only one portfolio holding record is missing or cannot be identified, then you do not have a valid portfolio collection.

The collection validation check means confirming that, for a given point in time, all required data records exist and are identifiable for a given collection (e.g., portfolio, index, ETF).

These codes are used to specify the data quality tolerance for the collection dimension, at the datum level:

V = Valid/within tolerance
  Means all components of the collection (e.g., portfolio positions, index constituents) exist and are identifiable

IV = Invalid/out of tolerance
  Means one or more components of the collection do not exist or are not identifiable

The collection validation check, while simple in concept and application, is extremely important in the financial industry. Collections such as portfolios, ETF, and indices *must* be complete to be useful. You cannot accurately calculate the net asset value of a portfolio if one or more portfolio holdings are missing. You cannot accurately use the weights of index or ETF constituents if one or more constituents are missing.

Example

The index record control count for the S&P 500 is 500. If you validate the index constituent records for a specific date and the number of constituent records equals 485, then you have an invalid S&P 500 index collection. Likewise, if you validate all portfolio holdings for an account for a specific date and the sum of the market values equals $654,341,899.00, and you know the valid account holdings market value control amount is $654,345,234.00, then you have an invalid portfolio holdings collection.

The collection validation check is used to verify all components of the collection exist and are identifiable. This check does not validate the datum values of the data components. You will need to use one or more of the other data dimension validation checks to validate the datum values of the collection.

Cohesion

The *cohesion* data dimension refers to the relationship between datum values that are typically organized as logical records. Generally, all datum values have a relationship to some other datum. This means the datum values must be organized and, at a minimum, paired with some form of identifier that links one datum, or dataset, to another and facilitates joining two or more datasets using the identifier. The identifier is often referred to as a *primary key* or as a *foreign key*. The identifier may be one datum value or it may be a combination of datum values. For example, since most of the data used in the financial industry is panel data volumes, then there is typically a date or date-time data element that would be used *along with the identifier* to uniquely identify a data record at a specific point in time. In either case, the objective is to establish a precise relationship that enables you to join data together. This is data cohesion.

Example

The ticker symbol AAPL refers to the issuer Apple Inc. The close price for a given date is $130.10 on 06/15/22. A valid identifier is required to indicate the close price of $130.10 on 06/15/22 is indeed the close price for Apple. Therefore, the data record must include the ticker symbol AAPL along with the close price and date to establish the relationship of these datum values for a specific date to the issuer Apple.

The cohesion validation check is used to confirm the identifiers for datum values in a data volume are valid and can be used to successfully link or join to other datum values in another data volume. The identifiers are often referred to as primary and foreign data keys between the data volumes. Security identifiers such as CUSIP, SEDOL, ISIN, account numbers, and unique system-generated record identifiers are all examples of identifiers used as primary and foreign keys between data volumes.

Identifiers such as CUSIP, SEDOL, and ISIN are not guaranteed to be unique over time. For example, the CUSIP used to identify a stock on a stock exchange is unique only if you include the exchange as part of the primary key since the CUSIP for a stock can be the same across many stock exchanges. Some of these identifiers can change over time. This presents yet a different problem, whereby the identifier that uniquely identified a stock was valid 10 years ago but became inactive due to delisting or corporate actions. However, recently a new identifier may be used to identify a completely different stock (yet one that has a lineage relationship to the prior company and identifier). This means using these industry-recognized security identifiers as primary and foreign data keys in historical time series cross-section data can be problematic. You are encouraged to use system-generated identifiers where feasible. This way, you can control both the logic used to create the unique data identification and the lineage of the data scheme for your data volumes.

These codes are used to specify the data quality tolerance for the cohesion dimension, at the datum level:

V = Valid/within tolerance
Means the identifiers are valid and can be used to join data across datasets

IV = Invalid/out of tolerance
Means one or more identifiers are invalid and cannot be used to join data across datasets

The cohesion validation check ensures different data volumes can be linked together. This is especially important in the financial industry since large time series, cross-section data volumes such as portfolio holdings, market data, fundamentals, and so on are commonly used. You must be able to uniquely identify and correctly link data records across multiple data volumes for the data to be useful.

Duplicates

Duplication, or multiple instances of the exact same datum value(s), is not a dimension of a datum. A duplicate datum or dataset (e.g., a data record) in a data volume is an additional instance of the same data in the data volume. Duplication is most often caused by a process or logic error. For example, running the same software application process to generate a set of data multiple times may result in multiple (duplicate) instances of the same data records being stored in the same data volume.

Regardless of the root cause, duplicate data in a data volume should be considered *corrupted* data. Data duplication checks are necessary to ensure the data volume is free from duplicates. You will see in later chapters how master data management and primary and foreign keys in data structures typically prevent duplication of data.

Summary

The data dimensions of completeness, timeliness, accuracy, precision, conformity, congruence, collection, and cohesion can be measured using simple mathematics and textual comparison techniques. The metrics generated from the measurements can be compared to the DQS of the consumer. You can deliver higher quality data by engineering and integrating pre-use data validations into data management processing pipelines to check data *before* it is provided to consumers. The next chapter provides detailed examples of the application of the DQS framework to data volumes. You will learn how data quality tolerances are defined in DQS and how they are used to measure data quality and generate data quality metrics.

CHAPTER 4

DQS Model Example

This chapter will demonstrate the use of the DQS framework. This framework defines the data quality tolerances for applicable dimensions for data in data volumes, as required by business functions. The model illustrated in Figure 4-1 is presented like a manufacturing assembly line, with 11 business functions shown from left to right. This is a simple model that provides sufficient details to illustrate the DQS framework and the concept of fit-for-purpose data. Your firm is likely organized differently, with different business functions, applications, and data requirements per function. The model illustrates the DQS for a subset of data volumes intended for use by downstream consumers and does not fully illustrate all DQS requirements for every function.

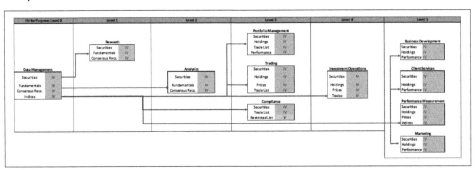

Figure 4-1. DQS model (large format, color version (https://oreil.ly/dqef-4-01))

You can use this model as a template and create a similar model to reflect your business functions, data requirements, and the DQS for data volumes you use or that your business functions or applications use. You can also apply this model more broadly to data that is used by many business functions and applications across your firm.

The business functions in this model are defined as follows:

Data Management function
> Ingests volumes of data from third-party data vendors and applies data quality validations to the data according to the DQS of downstream functions; remediates any data anomalies

Research function
> Receives data from the Data Management function and uses the data in investment research processes

Analytics function
> Receives data from the Data Management function and uses the data to generate security analytics data

Portfolio Management function
> Receives data from the Data Management, Research, Analytics, and Investment Operations functions to manage portfolios

Trading function
> Receives data from the Data Management function and uses the data to identify the securities for trading

Compliance function
> Receives data from the Data Management function and uses the data to identify the securities that have been traded; compares to client-restricted lists

Investment Operations function
> Receives data from the Data Management function and uses the data to identify securities and associated market data for accounting purposes

Business Development function
> Receives data from the Data Management function and uses the data to support generation of sales presentations

Client Services function
> Receives data from the Data Management function and uses the data to support client reporting

Performance Measurement function
> Receives data from the Data Management function and uses the data to calculate performance returns and attributions

Marketing function
> Receives data from the Data Management function and uses the data to generate marketing materials

Each business function is represented by a box. The box contains one or more data volumes required by the function to operate. The data quality status is indicated with a V (valid), IV (invalid), or S (suspect) based on the data quality metrics of the data volumes.

Figure 4-1 shows how the security master data is provisioned to the other downstream consumers from the Data Management function. You will see throughout the DQS model example how the application of DQS provide precise data quality measurements and metrics. The data quality metrics are used to determine if the data is fit for purpose and consumption by the business function. The *fit-for-purpose level*, explained later in this chapter, indicates different DQS tolerances for data used by business functions and applications. For example, a data volume containing stock prices with empty or stale values may be fit for purpose and usable for general investment research and stock market analysis, but empty prices are not fit for purpose for use by operations to calculate a portfolio's net asset value, nor by performance measurement to precisely calculate portfolio returns.

Figure 4-2 shows the uncleansed, raw dataset that will be used by the model to generate the data quality metrics for dimensions of completeness, timeliness, accuracy, precision, and conformity. This data volume is received by the Data Management function. This function applies data quality validations to the data volume based on the DQS of downstream consumers (e.g., Research, Analytics, Portfolio Management, and Trading functions). The Data Management function uses the data quality tolerances defined in the DQS to identify and correct the data anomalies.

Record	Processing Date	Ticker	Issue Name	Exchange	Bid	Ask	Spread	Market Cap	Market Cap Scale	PE	Consensus Recommendation	Consensus Date
1	10/26/2015	IBM	International Business Machines Corp	NYSE	139.02	140.82	1.8	136.62	B	9.65	1	10/5/2015
2	10/26/2015	AMGN	Amgen Inc.		158	165	7	123.34	B	21.55	1	10/5/2015
3	10/26/2015	AAPL	Apple Inc.	NASDAQ	118.27	120.69	2.42	664.97	B	13.79	1	10/5/2015
4	10/26/2015	WMTT1	Wal-Mart Stores, Inc.	NYSE	57.48		-57.48	184.79	B	12.05	0	10/5/2015
5	10/26/2015		Coca-Cola Company (The)	NYSE		42.9	42.9	185.83	B	25.06	1	10/5/2015
6	10/27/2015	IBM	International Business Machines Corp	NYSE	140.01	141.15	1.144	136.62	B	9.65	1	6/10/2015
7	10/27/2015	AMGN	Amgen Inc.		158	167	9	123.34		21.55	2	6/10/2015
8	10/27/2015	AAPL	Apple Inc.	NASDAQ	118.28		-118.28	664.97	B	13.79	1	6/10/2015
9	10/27/2015	WMT		NYSE	57.48	59.23	1.75	184.79	B	12.05	1	6/10/2015
10	10/27/2015	KO	Coca-Cola Company (The)	NYSE	0	43.2	43.2	185.83			5	6/10/2015
11	10/28/2015	IBM	INTERNATIONAL BUSINESS MACHINES COI	NYSE	139.02	143.22	4.2	136.62	B	9.65	1	9/1/2015
12	10/28/2015	AMGN	Amgen Inc.		159.12	163.12	4	123.34	B	21.55	2	10/7/2015
13	10/28/2015		APPLE	NASDAQ			0	664.97	B	13.8		10/7/1900
14	10/28/2015	WMT	Wal-Mart Stores, Inc.	NYSE	57.48	59.12	1.64	##########	B	1205	1	10/7/2015
15	10/28/2015	KO	Coca-Cola Company (The)	NYSE	4.12	42	37.88	185.83	B		1	10/7/2015
16	10/29/2015	IBM	International Business Machines Corp	NYSE	139.02	140.22	1.2	136.62	B	9.65	2	9/1/2015
17	10/29/2015	AMGN			158	162	4	123.34	S	21.55	1	10/8/2015
18	10/29/2015	AAPL	Apple Inc.	NASDAQ	118.27	119.46	1.19	664.97	B	13.79		10/8/2015
19	10/29/2015		Wal-Mart Stores, Inc.	NYSE	57.48	59.55	2.07	##########	B	1205	1	10/8/2015
20	10/29/2015	KO	Coke		42.34	45.99	3.65	185.83	B			
21	10/30/2015	IBM	IBM INC	NYSE	139.02		-139.02	136.62	B	9.65		9/1/2015
22	10/30/2015	AMGN	Amgen Inc.	NASDAQ	159	163.25	4.25	123.34	B	21.55	1	10/9/2015
23	10/30/2015	AAPL		NASDAQ	117.49	124.89	7.4	664970.00	B	13.79	-5	10/9/2015
24	10/30/2015	WMT	Walmart	NYSE	57.22	58.44	1.22	184.79	B	12.05	1	10/9/2015
25	10/30/2015	KO	Coca-Cola Company (The)	NYSE	40.24	41.88	1.64	185.83	B	25.06	1	10/9/2015

Figure 4-2. Raw security master data volume (large format, color version (https://oreil.ly/dqef-4-02))

Completeness DQS

As I've mentioned in earlier chapters, you need to determine whether the existence of the data is mandatory or optional. Every datum has a completeness or existence dimension. This is the most basic test for any piece of data. When data elements are defined as nonnullable (cannot be empty) in physical data structures such as databases, then the technology enforces completeness for those data elements in data volumes.

The completeness DQS for all data elements in the security master data volume are the same for each downstream business function. Table 4-1 outlines the data quality tolerances for each data element, defined by the DQS and required by all downstream consumers.

Table 4-1. Completeness DQS

Data element	Data quality description	DQS	Business impact
Ticker	All Ticker datum values are mandatory and cannot be empty; if any are empty, then the business impact is high.	Ticker: Completeness = M, IV ≥ 1, H	High
Issue Name	All Issue Name datum values are mandatory and cannot be empty; if any are empty, then the business impact is high.	Issue Name: Completeness = M, IV ≥ 1, H	High
Exchange	All Exchange symbol datum values are mandatory and cannot be empty; if any are empty, then the business impact is high.	Exchange: Completeness = M, IV ≥ 1, H	High
Bid	All Bid price datum values are mandatory and cannot be empty; if any are empty, then the business impact is high.	Bid: Completeness = M, IV ≥ 1, H	High
Ask	All Ask price datum values are mandatory and cannot be empty; if any are empty, then the business impact is high.	Ask: Completeness = M, IV ≥ 1, H	High
Spread	All Spread datum values are mandatory and cannot be empty; if any are empty, then the business impact is high.	Spread: Completeness = M, IV ≥ 1, H	High
Market Cap	All Market Cap datum values are mandatory and cannot be empty; if any are empty, then the business impact is high.	Market Cap: Completeness = M, IV ≥ 1, H	High
Market Cap Scale	All Market Cap Scale datum values are mandatory and cannot be empty; if any are empty, then the business impact is high.	Market Cap Scale: Completeness = M, IV ≥ 1, H	High
Price to Earnings (PE)	All PE datum values are mandatory and cannot be empty; if any are empty, then the business impact is high.	PE: Completeness = M, IV ≥ 1, H	High

Data element	Data quality description	DQS	Business impact
Consensus Recommendation	Consensus Recommendation datum values may or may not exist for a stock of an issuer; therefore, the existence of the Consensus Recommendation is optional and business impact is low.	Consensus Recommendation: Completeness = 0, S ≥ 1, L	Low
Consensus Date	Consensus Date datum values may or may not exist for a stock of an issuer; therefore, the existence of the Consensus Date is optional and business impact is low.	Consensus Date: Completeness = 0, S ≥ 1, L	Low

The model applies the completeness DQS to each datum in the security master data volume. Figure 4-3 illustrates the results and demonstrates the valid, invalid, or suspect data quality metric for each datum. The DQS indicate the Ticker, Issue Name, Exchange, Bid, Ask, Spread, Market Cap, Market Cap Scale, and PE datum values are mandatory and the data must exist. The DQS indicate the existence of Consensus Recommendation and Consensus Date datum values is optional. The model then generates the data quality metrics assigning datum values with V (valid) if the data exists, IV (invalid) if the data is empty, and S (suspect) if the data does not exist but the existence of the data is optional and not mandatory.

Record	Processing Date	Ticker	Issue Name	Exchange	Bid	Ask	Spread	Market Cap	Market Cap Scale	PE	Consensus Recom	Consensus Date
1	10/26/2015	V	V	V	V	V	V	V	V	V	V	V
2	10/26/2015	V	V	IV	V	V	V	V	V	V	V	V
3	10/26/2015	V	V	V	V	V	V	V	V	V	V	V
4	10/26/2015	V	V	V	V	IV	V	V	V	V	V	V
5	10/26/2015	IV	V	V	IV	V	V	V	V	V	V	V
6	10/27/2015	V	V	V	V	V	V	V	V	V	V	V
7	10/27/2015	V	V	IV	V	V	V	V	IV	V	V	V
8	10/27/2015	V	V	V	V	IV	V	V	V	V	V	V
9	10/27/2015	V	IV	V	V	V	V	V	V	V	V	V
10	10/27/2015	V	V	V	V	V	V	V	IV	IV	V	V
11	10/28/2015	V	V	V	V	V	V	V	V	V	V	V
12	10/28/2015	V	V	IV	V	V	V	V	V	V	V	V
13	10/28/2015	IV	V	V	IV	IV	V	V	V	V	S	V
14	10/28/2015	V	V	V	V	V	V	V	V	V	V	V
15	10/28/2015	V	V	V	V	V	V	V	V	IV	V	V
16	10/29/2015	V	V	V	V	V	V	V	V	V	V	V
17	10/29/2015	V	IV	V	IV	V	V	V	V	V	V	V
18	10/29/2015	V	V	V	V	V	V	V	V	V	S	V
19	10/29/2015	IV	V	V	V	V	V	V	V	V	V	V
20	10/29/2015	V	V	IV	V	V	V	V	V	IV	S	S
21	10/30/2015	V	V	V	V	IV	V	V	V	V	S	V
22	10/30/2015	V	V	V	V	V	V	V	V	V	V	V
23	10/30/2015	V	IV	V	V	V	V	V	V	V	V	V
24	10/30/2015	V	V	V	V	V	V	V	V	V	V	V
25	10/30/2015	V	V	V	V	V	V	V	V	V	V	V

Figure 4-3. Completeness data quality metrics (large format, color version (https://oreil.ly/dqef-4-03))

The application of the DQS for the completeness data dimension to the security master data volume generates both statistics and data quality metrics. The statistics for the security master data volume in Figure 4-3 are as follows:

- 25 datum records
- 11 data elements or columns (Ticker, Issue Name)
- 275 datum values that may or may not exist

Table 4-2 provides the total number of valid, invalid, and suspect metrics for the security master data volume.

Table 4-2. Summary of completeness data quality metrics

Data element	Valid	Invalid	Suspect
Ticker	22	3	0
Issue Name	22	3	0
Exchange	20	5	0
Bid	23	2	0
Ask	21	4	0
Spread	25	0	0
Market Cap	25	0	0
Market Cap Scale	23	2	0
Price to Earnings (PE)	22	3	0
Consensus Recommendation	21	0	4
Consensus Date	24	0	1
Metrics totals	**248**	**22**	**5**

Timeliness DQS

The timeliness DQS are the same for each downstream business function and are defined for the Consensus Date data element in the security master data volume in this model. Table 4-3 outlines the data quality tolerances for the timeliness data dimensions of the Consensus Date data element.

Table 4-3. Timeliness DQS

Data element	Data quality description	DQS	Business impact
Consensus Date	Consensus Date datum values may or may not exist for a stock of an issuer. If the date exists, then the Consensus Date is valid if the number of days between the Consensus Date and the Processing Date is less than 30, suspect if the number of days between the Consensus Date and the Processing Date is greater than or equal to 30 but less than 90, and invalid if the number of days is greater than or equal to 90. In all cases, the business impact is low.	Consensus Date: Timeliness = V < 30 days, 30 days ≤ S < 90, IV ≥ 90, L	Low

The model applies the timeliness DQS to the Consensus Date data element for each Consensus Date datum in the security master data volume. Figure 4-4 illustrates the results and shows the valid, invalid, or suspect data quality metric for each Consensus Date datum.

The DQS indicate the consensus date must be less than 30 days from the Processing Date to be valid, 30 days up to 90 days from the Processing Date to be suspect, and greater than or equal to 90 days from the Processing Date to be invalid. Figure 4-4 includes two new columns for illustration purposes: a copy of the Consensus Date datum values in the column named "Consensus Date2" and a column named "Number of Days," which represents the Consensus Date subtracted from the Processing Date. The model applies the DQS to the data volume and generates the data quality metrics illustrating Consensus Date datum values with V (valid) if the Consensus Date is less than 30 days from the Processing Date, IV (invalid) if the Consensus Date is greater than or equal to 90 days from the Processing Date, and S (suspect) if the Consensus Date is less than 90 but greater than or equal to 30 days from the Processing Date.

Record	Processing Date	Consensus Date	Consensus Date2	Number of Days
1	10/26/2015	V	10/5/2015	21
2	10/26/2015	V	10/5/2015	21
3	10/26/2015	V	10/5/2015	21
4	10/26/2015	V	10/5/2015	21
5	10/26/2015	V	10/5/2015	21
6	10/27/2015	IV	6/10/2015	139
7	10/27/2015	IV	6/10/2015	139
8	10/27/2015	IV	6/10/2015	139
9	10/27/2015	IV	6/10/2015	139
10	10/27/2015	IV	6/10/2015	139
11	10/28/2015	S	9/1/2015	57
12	10/28/2015	V	10/7/2015	21
13	10/28/2015	IV	10/7/1900	42,024
14	10/28/2015	V	10/7/2015	21
15	10/28/2015	V	10/7/2015	21
16	10/29/2015	S	9/1/2015	58
17	10/29/2015	V	10/8/2015	21
18	10/29/2015	V	10/8/2015	21
19	10/29/2015	V	10/8/2015	21
20	10/29/2015	S		42,306
21	10/30/2015	S	9/1/2015	59
22	10/30/2015	V	10/9/2015	21
23	10/30/2015	V	10/9/2015	21
24	10/30/2015	V	10/9/2015	21
25	10/30/2015	V	10/9/2015	21

Figure 4-4. Timeliness data quality metrics (large format, color version (https://oreil.ly/dqef-4-04))

Applying the DQS for the timeliness data dimension to the Consensus Date in the security master data volume generates both statistics and data quality metrics. The statistics for the security master data volume in Figure 4-4 are as follows:

- 25 datum records
- 1 data element (Consensus Date)
- 25 datum values

Table 4-4 shows the total number of valid, invalid, and suspect Consensus Date datum values in the security master data volume.

Table 4-4. Summary of timeliness data quality metrics

Data element	Valid	Invalid	Suspect
Consensus Date	15	6	4

Accuracy DQS

The accuracy DQS are the same for each downstream business function and are defined for the Ticker, Issue Name, and Exchange data elements in the security master data volume in this model. Table 4-5 outlines the data quality tolerances, as defined by the DQS, for the Ticker, Issue Name, and Exchange data elements. The official NYSE and NASDAQ security listing datasets are used by the model as authoritative sources to confirm the accuracy of the Ticker, Issue Name, and Exchange datum values in the security master data volume.

Table 4-5. Accuracy DQS

Data element	Data quality description	DQS	Business impact
Ticker	Ticker datum values must exist for a given issue. Use the Exchange datum to select either the NYSE or NASDAQ official listing dataset and match the Ticker. If the Ticker matches a Ticker in the applicable NYSE or NASDAQ dataset, then the Ticker is valid. If the Ticker does not match a Ticker in the official listings, then the Ticker is invalid and business impact is high.	Ticker: Accuracy— authoritative = V, Ticker = Ticker, IV, Ticker ≠ Ticker, H	High
Issue Name	Issue Name datum values must exist for a given issue. Use the Exchange datum to select either the NYSE or NASDAQ official listing dataset and match the Issue Name. If the Issue Name matches an Issue Name in the applicable NYSE or NASDAQ dataset, then the Issue Name is valid. If the Issue Name does not match an Issue Name in the official listings, then the Issue Name is invalid and business impact is high.	Issue Name: Accuracy— authoritative = V, Issue Name = Issue Name, IV, Issue Name ≠ Issue Name, H	High

Data element	Data quality description	DQS	Business impact
Exchange	Exchange datum values must exist for a given issue. The exchange is used to select the specific Exchange securities list to validate the Ticker and the Issue Name. If the Exchange is empty, then the Exchange, Ticker, and Issue Name are invalid. If the Exchange datum value matches either NYSE or NASDAQ, then the Exchange is valid. If the Exchange does not match NYSE or NASDAQ, then the Exchange is invalid and business impact is high.	Exchange: Accuracy— authoritative = V, Exchange = NYSE or NASDAQ, IV, Exchange ≠ NYSE or NASDAQ, H	High

The model applies the DQS to the Ticker, Issue Name, and Exchange data elements for each datum in the security master data volume. The model uses the data illustrated in Table 4-6. This dataset is an example of an authoritative source used during accuracy validation.

Table 4-6. Example NYSE and NASDAQ official securities list

Exchange	Ticker	Issue Name
NASDAQ	AAPL	Apple Inc.
NYSE	IBM	International Business Machines Corporation
NASDAQ	AMGN	Amgen Inc.
NYSE	WMT	Walmart Inc.
NYSE	KO	Coca-Cola Company (The)

The model applies the DQS to the Ticker, Issue Name, and Exchange data elements for each datum respectively in the security master data volume. Figure 4-5 illustrates the results and shows the valid, invalid, or suspect data quality metric for each datum. The DQS indicates the Ticker, Issue Name, and Exchange must match the Ticker, Issue Name, and Exchange in the official securities list to be valid. The Exchange is used to select the specific official exchange securities list to validate the Ticker and the Issue Name. If the Exchange datum is empty, then the Exchange, Ticker, and Issue Name are invalid. If any of the datum values do not match their respective data element in the official securities list, then the data is invalid.

Figure 4-5 includes three new columns for illustration purposes: a copy of the Ticker datum values in the column named "Ticker2," Issue Name datum values in the column named "Issue Name2," and Exchange datum values in the column named "Exchange2." The model applies the DQS to the data volume and generates the data quality metrics, assigning Ticker, Issue Name, and Exchange datum values with V (valid) if they match the official securities list or IV (invalid) if they do not match the official securities list.

Record	Processing Date	Ticker	Issue Name	Exchange	Ticker2	Issue Name2	Exchange2
1	10/26/2015	V	IV	V	IBM	International Business Machines Corp	NYSE
2	10/26/2015	IV	IV	IV	AMGN	Amgen Inc.	
3	10/26/2015	V	V	V	AAPL	Apple Inc.	NASDAQ
4	10/26/2015	IV	V	V	WMTTT	Wal-Mart Stores, Inc.	NYSE
5	10/26/2015	IV	V	V		Coca-Cola Company (The)	NYSE
6	10/27/2015	V	IV	V	IBM	International Business Machines Corp	NYSE
7	10/27/2015	IV	IV	IV	AMGN	Amgen Inc.	
8	10/27/2015	V	V	V	AAPL	Apple Inc.	NASDAQ
9	10/27/2015	V	IV	V	WMT		NYSE
10	10/27/2015	V	V	V	KO	Coca-Cola Company (The)	NYSE
11	10/28/2015	V	IV	V	IBM	INTERNATIONAL BUSINESS MACHINES CORP	NYSE
12	10/28/2015	IV	IV	IV	AMGN	Amgen Inc.	
13	10/28/2015	IV	IV	V		APPLE	NASDAQ
14	10/28/2015	V	V	V	WMT	Wal-Mart Stores, Inc.	NYSE
15	10/28/2015	V	V	V	KO	Coca-Cola Company (The)	NYSE
16	10/29/2015	V	IV	V	IBM	International Business Machines Corp	NYSE
17	10/29/2015	IV	IV	IV	AMGN		
18	10/29/2015	V	V	V	AAPL	Apple Inc.	NASDAQ
19	10/29/2015	IV	V	V		Wal-Mart Stores, Inc.	NYSE
20	10/29/2015	IV	IV	IV	KO	Coke	
21	10/30/2015	V	IV	V	IBM	IBM INC	NYSE
22	10/30/2015	V	V	V	AMGN	Amgen Inc.	NASDAQ
23	10/30/2015	V	IV	V	AAPL		NASDAQ
24	10/30/2015	V	IV	V	WMT	Walmart	NYSE
25	10/30/2015	V	V	V	KO	Coca-Cola Company (The)	NYSE

Figure 4-5. Accuracy data quality metrics (large format, color version (https://oreil.ly/dqef-4-05))

Applying the DQS for the accuracy data dimension to the Ticker, Issue Name, and Exchange in the security master data volume generates both statistics and data quality metrics. The statistics for the security master data volume in Figure 4-5 are as follows:

- 25 datum records
- 3 data elements (Ticker, Issue Name, and Exchange)
- 75 datum values

Table 4-7 provides the total number of valid, invalid, and suspect Ticker, Issue Name, and Exchange datum values in the security master data volume.

Table 4-7. Summary of accuracy data quality metrics

Data element	Valid	Invalid	Suspect
Ticker	16	9	0
Issue Name	11	14	0
Exchange	20	5	0
Metrics totals	47	28	0

By using the accuracy data validation check, there are several data anomalies that can be identified in the security master data volume, including empty Exchange datums, malformed Issue Name datums, and empty or malformed Ticker datum values.

Precision DQS

The precision data dimension in this framework refers to the scale of the number that confers how precise it is. Data types such as integers are whole numbers and do not have decimals. Data types such as decimals and floating points are numbers that have decimals. When numbers with decimals are defined for data elements in physical data structures, such as databases, then the technology enables them to be stored and expressed in the data volumes. However, the physical data element definition of decimal or floating point does not enforce an explicit number of decimals. Instead, the data type definitions for these numeric data types in the physical technology allow a maximum number of decimals to be stored. Decimal data types define a specific, maximum number of decimals. Therefore, if the DQS require five decimals and the data type is defined with two decimals, then you will lose precision (dropped decimal values) when storing a five-decimal number in a two-decimal physical data typed structure. Floating point data types present a different challenge. Numbers with decimals resulting from calculations that are stored in floating point data type structures do not have an exact binary representation at the compute level. The implications can be inaccurate representation of the number as a stored value, thus potential loss of precision, potential mismatch of floating point numbers to other numeric data types, and the results of calculations may yield extraneous decimals (which, when used in combinatorial or compounding calculations may yield highly inaccurate results). This means if your DQS require a specific number of decimals, then you need to validate the precision using a validation check.

As mentioned in Chapter 3, precision and precision misalignment are often overlooked due to the complexities of storing and processing numbers using diverse data structures in databases with data typed columns and data type objects in programming languages. You need to ensure the precision required in the DQS for a consumer or application is consistent throughout the data structures and data processing applications.

The precision DQS are the same for each downstream business function and are defined for the Bid, Ask, Spread, and PE data elements in the security master data volume in this model. Table 4-8 outlines the data quality tolerances for the Bid, Ask, Spread, and PE data elements.

Table 4-8. Precision DQS

Data element	Data quality description	DQS	Business impact
Bid	All Bid price datum values are mandatory. If the Bid price datum is empty or a negative number, then it is invalid. If the decimal is missing, then it is suspect. If the number of decimals is greater than or equal to one, then it is valid, and business impact is high.	Bid: Precision—decimal $= V \geq 1, S = 0, IV =$ negative, H	High
Ask	All Ask price datum values are mandatory. If the Ask price datum is empty or a negative number, then it is invalid. If the decimal is missing, then it is suspect. If the number of decimals is greater than or equal to one, then it is valid, and business impact is high.	Ask: Precision—decimal $= V \geq 1, S = 0, IV =$ negative, H	High
Spread	All Spread datum values are mandatory. If the Spread datum is empty or a negative number, then it is invalid. If the decimal is missing, then it is suspect. If the number of decimals is greater than or equal to one, then it is valid, and business impact is high.	Spread: Precision—decimal $= V \geq 1, S = 0,$ $IV =$ negative, H	High
Price to Earnings (PE)	All PE datum values are mandatory. If the PE datum is empty or a negative number, then it is invalid. If the decimal is missing, then it is suspect. If the number of decimals is greater than or equal to one, then it is valid, and business impact is high.	PE: Precision—decimal $= V \geq 1, S = 0, IV =$ negative, H	High

The model applies the precision DQS to the Bid, Ask, Spread, and PE data elements for each datum in the security master data volume. Figure 4-6 illustrates the results and shows the valid, invalid, or suspect data quality metric for each Bid, Ask, Spread, and PE datum.

The DQS indicate the precision of the Bid, Ask, Spread, and PE datum values is based on the following: datum values must have one or more decimals to be valid, missing decimals are suspect, and negative numbers are invalid. Figure 4-6 includes four new columns for illustration purposes: one copy each of the Bid, Ask, Spread, and PE datum values in the columns named "Bid2," "Ask2," "Spread2," and "PE2." The model applies the DQS to the data volume and generates the data quality metrics illustrating the datum values with V (valid) if the numbers exist, are not negative numbers, and have one or more decimals; S (suspect) if the numbers exist, are not negative, and lack a decimal; and IV (invalid) if the numbers either do not exist or are negative numbers.

The application of the DQS for the precision data dimension to the Bid, Ask, Spread, and PE in the security master data volume generates both statistics and data quality metrics. The statistics for the security master data volume in Figure 4-6 are as follows:

- 25 datum records
- 4 data elements (Bid, Ask, Spread, and PE)
- 100 datum values

Record	Processing Date	Bid	Ask	Spread	PE	Bid2	Ask2	Spread2	PE2
1	10/26/2015	V	V	V	V	139.02	140.82	1.8	9.65
2	10/26/2015	S	S	S	V	158	165	7	21.55
3	10/26/2015	V	V	V	V	118.27	120.69	2.42	13.79
4	10/26/2015	V	IV	IV	V	57.48		-57.48	12.05
5	10/26/2015	IV	V	V	V		42.9	42.9	25.06
6	10/27/2015	V	V	V	V	140.01	141.154	1.144	9.65
7	10/27/2015	S	S	S	V	158	167	9	21.55
8	10/27/2015	S	IV	IV	V	118.275		-118.275	13.79
9	10/27/2015	V	V	V	V	57.48	59.23	1.75	12.05
10	10/27/2015	S	V	V	IV	0	43.2	43.2	
11	10/28/2015	V	V	V	V	139.02	143.22	4.2	9.65
12	10/28/2015	V	V	S	V	159.12	163.12	4	21.55
13	10/28/2015	IV	IV	S	V			0	13.798
14	10/28/2015	V	V	V	S	57.48	59.12	1.64	1205
15	10/28/2015	V	S	V	IV	4.12	42	37.88	
16	10/29/2015	V	V	V	V	139.02	140.22	1.2	9.65
17	10/29/2015	S	S	S	V	158	162	4	21.55
18	10/29/2015	V	V	V	V	118.27	119.46	1.19	13.79
19	10/29/2015	V	V	V	S	57.48	59.55	2.07	1205
20	10/29/2015	V	V	V	IV	42.34	45.99	3.65	
21	10/30/2015	V	IV	IV	V	139.02		-139.02	9.65
22	10/30/2015	S	V	V	V	159	163.25	4.25	21.55
23	10/30/2015	V	V	V	V	117.49	124.89	7.4	13.79
24	10/30/2015	V	V	V	V	57.22	58.44	1.22	12.05
25	10/30/2015	V	V	V	V	40.24	41.88	1.64	25.06

Figure 4-6. Precision data quality metrics (large format, color version (https://oreil.ly/dqef-4-06))

Table 4-9 shows the total number of valid, invalid, and suspect Bid, Ask, Spread, and PE datum values in the security master data volume.

Table 4-9. Summary of precision data quality metrics

Data element	Valid	Invalid	Suspect
Bid	17	2	6
Ask	17	4	4
Spread	17	3	5
PE	20	3	2
Metrics totals	71	12	17

The precision data dimension for the Bid, Ask, Spread, and PE datum values validates the data exists and is not a negative number, and counts the number of decimals according to the DQS. By using the precision validation check, several data anomalies—including empty Bid, Ask, and PE datum values, missing decimals, and negative Spread datum values—can be identified in the security master data volume.

Conformity DQS

The conformity DQS are the same for each downstream business function and are defined for the Issue Name, Market Cap Scale, and the Consensus Recommendation data elements in the security master data volume in this model. Data types such as dates, timestamps, and date-times have specific formats. When these data types are defined for data elements in physical data structures, such as databases, then the technology enforces conformity for those data elements in the data volumes. Table 4-10 outlines the data quality tolerances for the Issue Name, Market Cap Scale, and Consensus Recommendation data elements.

Table 4-10. Conformity DQS

Data element	Data quality description	DQS	Business impact
Issue Name	All Issue Name datum values are mandatory and must be in proper case. If the Issue Name is empty or is entirely in uppercase or lowercase letters, then it is invalid, and business impact is high.	Issue Name: Conformity—letter case = V = proper case, IV = empty or uppercase or lowercase, H	High
Market Cap Scale	All Market Cap Scale datum values are mandatory and must be either uppercase B (that represents billion) or uppercase M (that represents million). If the Market Cap Scale is empty or any value other than uppercase B or uppercase M, then it is invalid, and business impact is high.	Market Cap Scale: Conformity = V = B or M, IV ≠ B or M, H	High
Consensus Recommendation	Consensus Recommendation datum values are optional and must be a number between negative three and three. If the Consensus Recommendation is empty, then it is suspect. If the Consensus Recommendation is any number less than negative three or greater than three, then it is invalid, and business impact is low.	Consensus Recommendation: Conformity = V ≥ -3 and ≤ 3, S = empty, IV < -3 and > 3, L	Low

The model applies the conformity DQS to the Issue Name, Market Cap, and Consensus Recommendation data elements for each datum in the security master data volume. Figure 4-7 illustrates the results and shows the valid, invalid, or suspect data quality metric for each Issue Name, Market Cap, and Consensus Recommendation datum.

The conformity DQS for Issue Name indicate the Issue Name datum values must be in proper case to be valid. Otherwise, if the datum values are empty or are in lowercase or uppercase letters, then they are invalid. The conformity DQS for Market Cap Scale indicate the Market Cap Scale datum values must be either B (billion) or M (million) to be valid. Otherwise, if the datum values are empty or are any other value, then they are invalid. The conformity DQS for Consensus Recommendation indicate the Consensus Recommendation datum values are optional and must be a number equal to or greater than -3 and less than or equal to 3 to be valid. Otherwise, if the datum values are empty or are any number less than -3 or greater than 3, then they are invalid. Figure 4-7 includes three new columns for illustration purposes: a copy each of the Issue Name, Market Cap, and Consensus Recommendation datum values in the columns named "Issue Name2," "Market Cap Scale2," and "Consensus Recommendation2."

Record	Processing Date	Issue Name	Market Cap Scale	Consensus Recommendation	Issue Name2	Market Cap Scale2	Consensus Recommendation2
1	10/26/2015	V	V	V	International Business Machines Corp	B	1
2	10/26/2015	V	V	V	Amgen Inc.	B	1
3	10/26/2015	V	V	V	Apple Inc.	B	1
4	10/26/2015	V	V	V	Wal-Mart Stores, Inc.	B	0
5	10/26/2015	V	V	V	Coca-Cola Company (The)	B	1
6	10/27/2015	V	V	V	International Business Machines Corp	B	1
7	10/27/2015	V	IV	V	Amgen Inc.		2
8	10/27/2015	V	V	V	Apple Inc.	B	1
9	10/27/2015	IV	V	V		B	1
10	10/27/2015	V	IV	IV	Coca-Cola Company (The)		5
11	10/28/2015	IV	V	V	INTERNATIONAL BUSINESS MACHINES CORP	B	1
12	10/28/2015	V	V	V	Amgen Inc.	B	2
13	10/28/2015	IV	V	S	APPLE	B	
14	10/28/2015	V	V	V	Wal-Mart Stores, Inc.	B	1
15	10/28/2015	V	V	V	Coca-Cola Company (The)	B	1
16	10/29/2015	V	V	V	International Business Machines Corp	B	2
17	10/29/2015	IV	IV	V		S	1
18	10/29/2015	V	V	S	Apple Inc.	B	
19	10/29/2015	V	V	V	Wal-Mart Stores, Inc.	B	1
20	10/29/2015	V	V	S	Coke	B	
21	10/30/2015	IV	V	S	IBM INC	B	
22	10/30/2015	V	V	V	Amgen Inc.	B	1
23	10/30/2015	IV	V	IV		B	-5
24	10/30/2015	V	V	V	Walmart	B	1
25	10/30/2015	V	V	V	Coca-Cola Company (The)	B	1

Figure 4-7. Conformity data quality metrics (large format, color version (https://oreil.ly/dqef-4-07))

The model applies the DQS to the data volume and generates the data quality metrics, assigning some datum values with V (valid), which means:

- The Issue Name datum exists and is in proper case
- The Market Cap Scale datum exists and is either uppercase B or uppercase M
- If the Consensus Recommendation datum exists, then the datum value is a number equal to or greater than -3 and less than or equal to 3

The model assigns S (suspect) only to the Consensus Recommendation datum values and indicates if the datum value does not exist.

The model assigns some datum values with IV (invalid), which means:

- The Issue Name datum does not exist or is not in proper case
- The Market Cap Scale datum does not exist or is not an uppercase B or an uppercase M
- If the Consensus Recommendation datum exists, then the datum value is not a number equal to or greater than -3 and less than or equal to 3

Applying the DQS for the conformity data dimension to the Issue Name, Market Cap Scale, and Consensus Recommendation in the security master data volume generates both statistics and data quality metrics. The statistics for the security master data volume in Figure 4-7 are as follows:

- 25 datum records
- 3 data elements (Issue Name, Market Cap Scale, and Consensus Recommendation)
- 75 datum values

Table 4-11 provides the total number of valid, invalid, and suspect Issue Name, Market Cap Scale, and Consensus Recommendation datum values in the security master data volume.

Table 4-11. Summary of conformity data quality metrics

Data element	Valid	Invalid	Suspect
Issue Name	19	6	0
Market Cap Scale	22	3	0
Consensus Recommendation	19	2	4
Metrics totals	60	11	4

The conformity data dimension for the Issue Name, Market Cap Scale, and Consensus Recommendation datum values is specific to each of the data elements. Therefore, the validation logic for each data element defined in the DQS is also specific to the data element.

By using the conformity data validation checks, several data anomalies—including empty Issue Name and Market Cap Scale datum values, malformed Issue Name datum values (e.g., values that appear in all uppercase letters), and invalid Market Cap Scale and Consensus Recommendation datum values—are identified in the security master data volume.

Congruence DQS

Chapter 3 introduced three types of congruence data quality checks: prior value comparison, comparison to average, and comparison to standard deviation z-score. As mentioned, I encourage you to develop your own congruence validation checks using more sophisticated logic that may be more applicable to the data you use.

Figure 4-8 shows 10 business days of cleansed Bid, Ask, and Spread data. The data volume has been validated using the DQS, and data validations have been applied to the data elements for completeness, timeliness, accuracy, precision, and conformity. The model uses this data to demonstrate the congruence DQS.

Record	Processing Date	Ticker	Bid	Ask	Spread
1	10/19/2015	IBM	139	140	0.96
2	10/19/2015	AMGN	158.7	165	6.3
3	10/19/2015	AAPL	118.5	120	1.57
4	10/19/2015	WMT	57.48	58.12	0.64
5	10/19/2015	KO	42.32	42.79	0.47
6	10/20/2015	IBM	139	140.7	1.62
7	10/20/2015	AMGN	160	164.8	4.77
8	10/20/2015	AAPL	118.4	119.9	1.54
9	10/20/2015	WMT	57.36	57.63	0.27
10	10/20/2015	KO	42.34	42.88	0.54
11	10/21/2015	IBM	138.5	140.8	2.29
12	10/21/2015	AMGN	160.3	164.9	4.63
13	10/21/2015	AAPL	119.7	120.2	0.54
14	10/21/2015	WMT	58.32	58.65	0.33
15	10/21/2015	KO	41.23	42.89	1.66
16	10/22/2015	IBM	139.2	140.3	1.12
17	10/22/2015	AMGN	159.6	165.6	5.98
18	10/22/2015	AAPL	118.6	120.5	1.89
19	10/22/2015	WMT	57.48	58.15	0.67
20	10/22/2015	KO	41.95	42.47	0.52
21	10/23/2015	IBM	139.5	140.8	1.36
22	10/23/2015	AMGN	158.9	165.3	6.33
23	10/23/2015	AAPL	118.4	120	1.63
24	10/23/2015	WMT	56.36	58.98	2.62
25	10/23/2015	KO	42.44	42.75	0.31
26	10/26/2015	IBM	139	140.8	1.79
27	10/26/2015	AMGN	158.9	165	6.07
28	10/26/2015	AAPL	118.3	120.7	2.42
29	10/26/2015	WMT	57.48	58.12	0.64
30	10/26/2015	KO	42.34	42.91	0.57
31	10/27/2015	IBM	140	141.1	1.04
32	10/27/2015	AMGN	158.9	167	8.07
33	10/27/2015	AAPL	118.3	122.6	4.28
34	10/27/2015	WMT	58.32	59.23	0.91
35	10/27/2015	KO	42.34	43.21	0.87
36	10/28/2015	IBM	139	143.2	4.19
37	10/28/2015	AMGN	159.6	163.8	4.22
38	10/28/2015	AAPL	117.6	119.3	1.71
39	10/28/2015	WMT	57.34	58.11	0.77
40	10/28/2015	KO	41.21	42.09	0.88

Figure 4-8. Extended security master data volume (large format, color version (https://oreil.ly/dqef-4-08))

The model applies the congruence DQS outlined in Table 4-12 to the uncleansed, raw market data illustrated in Figure 4-9.

Record	Processing Date	Ticker	Bid	Ask	Spread
51	11/2/15	IBM	133.31	134.22	0.91
52	11/2/15	AMGN	159.99	163.25	3.26
53	11/2/15	AAPL	117.49	124.88	7.39
54	11/2/15	WMT	57.29	57.61	0.32
55	11/2/15	KO	39.55	41.88	2.33

Figure 4-9. Raw market data

The congruence DQS are the same for each downstream business function and are defined for the Bid, Ask, and Spread data elements in the security master data volume. Table 4-12 outlines the data quality tolerances for the Bid price, Ask price, and Spread data elements—these elements are all specific to a given stock. For example, the raw Bid price for Apple (AAPL) in Figure 4-9 with Processing Date 11/2/2015 is $117.49, and the historical Bid prices for Apple (illustrated in Figure 4-8) are $118.45, $118.35, and so on. The historical Bid prices for Apple are used to validate the raw Apple Bid price in the congruence z-score data quality validation.

Table 4-12. Congruence z-score DQS

Data element	Data quality description	DQS	Business impact
Bid	All Bid price datum values are mandatory and historical Bid price sample range is 10 business days. If the z-score of the Bid price is equal to or less than three, then it is valid. If the Bid price z-score is greater than three but less than four, then it is suspect. If the Bid price z-score is equal to or greater than four, then it is invalid. In all cases, the business impact is high.	Bid: Congruence z-score = range 10 business days, V ≤ 3, S > 3 and < 4, H, IV ≥ 4, H	High
Ask	All Ask price datum values are mandatory and historical Ask price sample range is 10 business days. If the z-score of the Ask price is equal to or less than three, then it is valid. If the Ask price z-score is greater than three but less than four, then it is suspect. If the Ask price z-score is equal to or greater than four, then it is invalid. In all cases, the business impact is high.	Ask: Congruence z-score = range 10 business days, V ≤ 3, S > 3 and < 4, H, IV ≥ 4, H	High
Spread	All Spread datum values are mandatory and historical Spread sample range is 10 business days. If the z-score of the Spread is equal to or less than three, then it is valid. If the Spread z-score is greater than three but less than four, then it is suspect. If the Spread z-score is equal to or greater than four, then it is invalid. In all cases, the business impact is high.	Spread: Congruence z-score = range 10 business days, V ≤ 3, S > 3 and < 4, H, IV ≥ 4, H	High

The model applies the congruence DQS to the raw Bid, Ask, and Spread data elements for each datum in the raw market data volume. Tables 4-13 through 4-15 show the calculation statistics from the congruence z-score calculations.

Table 4-13. Bid price congruence z-score results

Processing date	Ticker	Bid	Mean bid (prior 10 days)	Bid standard deviation	Bid z-score
11/2/2015	AAPL	117.49	118.32	0.5646	1.48
11/2/2015	AMGN	159.99	159.38	0.5329	1.15
11/2/2015	IBM	133.31	139.13	0.3695	15.75
11/2/2015	KO	39.55	41.88	0.7014	3.31
11/2/2015	WMT	57.29	57.48	0.5260	0.37

Table 4-14. Ask price congruence z-score results

Processing date	Ticker	Ask	Mean ask (prior 10 days)	Ask standard deviation	Ask z-score
11/2/2015	AAPL	124.88	120.74	1.6289	2.54
11/2/2015	AMGN	163.25	164.74	1.1178	1.34
11/2/2015	IBM	134.22	141.08	1.0511	6.53
11/2/2015	KO	41.88	42.74	0.4692	1.84
11/2/2015	WMT	57.61	58.50	0.5668	1.57

Table 4-15. Spread congruence z-score results

Processing date	Ticker	Spread	Mean spread (prior 10 days)	Spread standard deviation	Spread z-score
11/2/2015	AAPL	7.39	2.41	1.9030	2.62
11/2/2015	AMGN	3.26	5.37	1.3561	1.55
11/2/2015	IBM	0.91	1.95	1.1270	0.93
11/2/2015	KO	2.33	0.87	0.4620	3.16
11/2/2015	WMT	0.32	1.01	0.7230	0.96

Figure 4-10 illustrates the results and shows the valid, invalid, or suspect data quality metric for each raw Bid price, Ask price, and Spread datum.

Record	Processing Date	Ticker	Bid	Ask	Spread	Z-Score Bid	Z-Score Ask	Z-Score Spread	Z-Score Bid	Z-Score Ask	Z-Score Spread
51	11/2/15	IBM	133.31	134.22	0.91	IV	IV	V	15.75	6.53	0.93
52	11/2/15	AMGN	159.99	163.25	3.26	V	V	V	1.15	1.34	1.55
53	11/2/15	AAPL	117.49	124.88	7.39	V	V	V	1.48	2.54	2.62
54	11/2/15	WMT	57.29	57.61	0.32	V	V	V	0.37	1.57	0.96
55	11/2/15	KO	39.55	41.88	2.33	S	V	S	3.31	1.84	3.16

Figure 4-10. Congruence z-score data quality metrics (large format, color version (https://oreil.ly/dqef-4-10))

The model applies the DQS to the raw data volume, using the historical data volume as reference, and generates the data quality metrics assigning the datum values with V (valid) if the z-score for the Bid, Ask, are Spread datum is equal to or less than three standard deviations from the mean; S (suspect) if the z-score for the Bid, Ask, or Spread datum is greater than three but less than four standard deviations from the mean; and IV (invalid) if the z-score for the Bid, Ask, or Spread datum is equal to or greater than four standard deviations from the mean. Figure 4-10 includes the z-scores for the raw Bid, Ask, and Spread datum values for illustration purposes.

The valid data quality metrics, shown in Figure 4-10, are as follows:

- The raw Bid price of $159.99 for Amgen (AMGN) on 11/2/2015 with a z-score of 1.15 is 1.15 standard deviations from the mean Bid price of $159.38 that is the average Amgen Bid price for the prior 10 days.

- The raw Bid price of $117.49 for Apple (AAPL) on 11/2/2015 with a z-score of 1.48 is 1.48 standard deviations from the mean Bid price of $118.32 that is the average Apple Bid price for the prior 10 days.

- The raw Bid price of $57.29 for Walmart (WMT) on 11/2/2015 with a z-score of 0.37 is 0.37 standard deviations from the mean Bid price of $57.48 that is the average Walmart Bid price for the prior 10 days.

- The raw Ask price of $163.25 for Amgen (AMGN) on 11/2/2015 with a z-score of 1.34 is 1.34 standard deviations from the mean Ask price of $164.74 that is the average Amgen Ask price for the prior 10 days.

- The raw Ask price of $124.88 for Apple (AAPL) on 11/2/2015 with a z-score of 2.54 is 2.54 standard deviations from the mean Ask price of $120.74 that is the average Apple Ask price for the prior ten days.

- The raw Ask price of $57.61 for Walmart (WMT) on 11/2/2015 with a z-score of 1.57 is 1.57 standard deviations from the mean Ask price of $58.50 that is the average Walmart Ask price for the prior 10 days.

- The raw Ask price of $41.88 for Coca-Cola (KO) on 11/2/2015 with a z-score of 1.84 is 1.84 standard deviations from the mean Ask price of $42.74 that is the average Coca-Cola Ask price for the prior 10 days.

- The raw Spread of $0.91 for International Business Machines (IBM) on 11/2/2015 with a z-score of 0.93 is 0.93 standard deviations from the mean Spread of $1.95 that is the average IBM Spread for the prior 10 days.

- The raw Spread of $3.26 for Amgen (AMGN) on 11/2/2015 with a z-score of 1.55 is 1.55 standard deviations from the mean Spread of $5.37 that is the average Amgen Spread for the prior 10 days.

- The raw Spread of $7.39 for Apple (AAPL) on 11/2/2015 with a z-score of 2.62 is 2.62 standard deviations from the mean Spread of $2.41 that is the average Apple Spread for the prior 10 days.

- The raw Spread of $0.32 for Walmart (WMT) on 11/2/2015 with a z-score of 0.96 is 0.96 standard deviations from the mean Spread of $1.01 that is the average Walmart Spread for the prior 10 days.

The suspect data quality metrics, as shown in Figure 4-10, are as follows:

- The raw Bid price of $39.55 for Coca-Cola (KO) on 11/2/2015 with a z-score of 3.31 is 3.31 standard deviations from the mean Bid price of $41.88 that is the average Coca-Cola Bid price for the prior 10 days.

- The raw Spread of $2.33 for Coca-Cola (KO) on 11/2/2015 with a z-score of 3.16 is 3.16 standard deviations from the mean Spread of $0.87 that is the average Coca-Cola Spread for the prior 10 days.

The invalid data quality metrics, as shown in Figure 4-10, are as follows:

- The raw Bid price of $133.31 for International Business Machines (IBM) on 11/2/2015 with a z-score of 15.75 is 15.75 standard deviations from the mean Bid price of $139.13 that is the average IBM Bid price for the prior 10 days.

- The raw Ask price of $134.22 for International Business Machines (IBM) on 11/2/2015 with a z-score of 6.53 is 6.53 standard deviations from the mean Ask price of $141.08 that is the average IBM Ask price for the prior 10 days.

Applying the DQS for the congruence data dimension to the Bid, Ask, and Spread datum values in the raw market data volume generates both statistics and data quality metrics. The statistics for the raw market data volume in Figure 4-10 are as follows:

- 5 datum records
- 3 data elements (Bid, Ask, and Spread)
- 15 datum values

Table 4-16 shows the total number of valid, invalid, and suspect Bid, Ask, and Spread datum values in the raw market data volume.

Table 4-16. Summary of congruence z-score data quality metrics

Data element	Valid	Invalid	Suspect
Bid	3	1	1
Ask	4	1	0
Spread	4	0	1
Metrics totals	11	2	2

The DQS for the congruence data dimension for Bid, Ask, and Spread datum values are specific to the stock (e.g., Apple, Walmart) and are relatable to historical Bid, Ask, and Spread datum observations. Therefore, you can use prior value comparison, comparison to average, or, as illustrated in this example, z-score to standardize the method of anomaly detection. This is a simple example to illustrate the statistical mechanics of the congruence z-score data quality validation. I encourage you to develop your own congruence validation checks and relevant data quality tolerances using more sophisticated logic that may be more applicable and useful to identify data anomalies relative to the nature of the data.

Eleven datum values are within the valid tolerance; however, several data anomalies are identified using the congruence z-score data quality validation as defined in the DQS that do not meet the valid tolerance condition. This statistical approach to data validation for time series datum values is useful to detect anomalies or outliers. These datum values may or may not be valid, but since their respective z-scores are not within the expected valid tolerance, they require further inspection and review.

The model uses the cleansed master data volume, illustrated in Figure 4-11, to remediate the data anomalies.

Record	Processing Date	Ticker	Issue Name	Exchange	Bid	Ask	Spread	Market Cap	Market Cap Scale	PE	Concensus Recommendation	Concensus Date
1	10/26/2015	IBM	International Business Machines Corporation	NYSE	139.02	140.81	1.79	136.62	B	9.65	1	10/22/2015
2	10/26/2015	AMGN	Amgen Inc.	NASDAQ	158.94	165.01	6.07	123.34	B	21.55	1	10/26/2015
3	10/26/2015	AAPL	Apple Inc.	NASDAQ	118.27	120.69	2.42	664.97	B	13.79	1	10/21/2015
4	10/26/2015	WMT	Wal-Mart Stores, Inc.	NYSE	57.48	58.12	0.64	184.79	B	12.05	1	10/26/2015
5	10/26/2015	KO	Coca-Cola Company (The)	NYSE	42.34	42.91	0.57	185.83	B	25.06	1	10/26/2015
6	10/27/2015	IBM	International Business Machines Corporation	NYSE	140.01	141.05	1.04	136.62	B	9.65	1	10/27/2015
7	10/27/2015	AMGN	Amgen Inc.	NASDAQ	158.94	167.01	8.07	123.34	B	21.55	2	10/27/2015
8	10/27/2015	AAPL	Apple Inc.	NASDAQ	118.27	122.55	4.28	664.97	B	13.79	1	10/15/2015
9	10/27/2015	WMT	Wal-Mart Stores, Inc.	NYSE	57.48	59.23	1.75	184.79	B	12.05	1	10/27/2015
10	10/27/2015	KO	Coca-Cola Company (The)	NYSE	42.34	43.21	0.87	185.83	B	25.06	1	10/27/2015
11	10/28/2015	IBM	International Business Machines Corporation	NYSE	139.02	143.21	4.19	136.62	B	9.65	1	10/28/2015
12	10/28/2015	AMGN	Amgen Inc.	NASDAQ	159.55	163.77	4.22	123.34	B	21.55	2	10/28/2015
13	10/28/2015	AAPL	Apple Inc.	NASDAQ	117.55	119.26	1.71	664.97	B	13.79	1	10/28/2015
14	10/28/2015	WMT	Wal-Mart Stores, Inc.	NYSE	57.48	58.11	0.63	184.79	B	12.05	1	10/28/2015
15	10/28/2015	KO	Coca-Cola Company (The)	NYSE	41.21	42.09	0.88	185.83	B	25.06	1	10/28/2015
16	10/29/2015	IBM	International Business Machines Corporation	NYSE	139.02	140.23	1.21	136.62	B	9.65	2	10/29/2015
17	10/29/2015	AMGN	Amgen Inc.	NASDAQ	158.94	162.98	4.04	123.34	B	21.55	1	10/29/2015
18	10/29/2015	AAPL	Apple Inc.	NASDAQ	118.27	119.42	1.15	664.97	B	13.79	1	10/29/2015
19	10/29/2015	WMT	Wal-Mart Stores, Inc.	NYSE	57.48	59.55	2.07	184.79	B	12.05		
20	10/29/2015	KO	Coca-Cola Company (The)	NYSE	42.34	45.99	3.65	185.83	B	25.06	1	10/29/2015
21	10/30/2015	IBM	International Business Machines Corporation	NYSE	139.02	142.98	3.96	136.62	B	9.65	2	10/30/2015
22	10/30/2015	AMGN	Amgen Inc.	NASDAQ	159.99	163.25	3.26	123.34	B	21.55	1	10/30/2015
23	10/30/2015	AAPL	Apple Inc.	NASDAQ	117.49	124.88	7.39	664970	M	13.79	1	10/30/2015
24	10/30/2015	WMT	Wal-Mart Stores, Inc.	NYSE	57.22	58.44	1.22	184.79	B	12.05	1	10/30/2015
25	10/30/2015	KO	Coca-Cola Company (The)	NYSE	40.24	41.88	1.64	185.83	B	25.06	1	10/30/2015

Figure 4-11. Cleansed security master data volume (large format, color version (https://oreil.ly/dqef-4-11))

After the data anomalies are corrected, a summary of data quality metrics is illustrated in Figure 4-12. This shows the data quality status for the securities data volume has changed from IV (invalid) to V (valid). This example illustrates the data quality of the securities, fundamentals, and prices data in the master data volume meets the DQS for all downstream consumers. However, there are still additional data anomalies to be corrected.

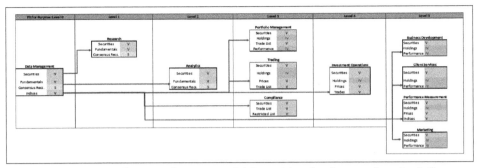

Figure 4-12. Data quality specification model (securities, fundamentals, prices) (large format, color version (https://oreil.ly/dqef-4-12))

Collection DQS

As we've discussed, a *data collection* is a discrete and distinct set of data, typically records of data, organized as a collection. All records must exist for a data collection to be a complete volume. The records in a data collection are a set of data elements (e.g., identifier, account, ticker, quantity, currency, weight). Indices, benchmarks, exchange-traded funds (ETF), and portfolio holdings are collections of data records that, respectively in aggregate, constitute data collections. The collection validation check entails validating all required data records exist for a specific point in time and are identifiable for a given collection (e.g., portfolio, index, ETF). There are many methods (from simple to sophisticated) that can be used to validate a data collection, including record counts, market value aggregation and comparison, and weights aggregation and comparison. As I've noted previously, you are encouraged to develop your own collection validation checks using additional tolerance ranges and more sophisticated logic that may be more applicable for the data you use.

Figure 4-13 represents five business days of cleansed Account, Account Name, Ticker, and Quantity data. This data volume also includes the validated Bid prices and the calculated Market Value for each portfolio holding. This data volume has already been validated using DQS and tolerances for completeness (relative to all the data elements), timeliness (for the Processing Date), conformity (for the Account, Account Name, and Ticker), and precision (for the Bid and Quantity). In addition, the portfolio collections (Voyager and Ping) have been validated for each day using collection DQS, confirming the historical portfolio holdings are complete and valid collections.

Record	Processing Date	Account	Account Name	Ticker	Quantity	Bid	Market Value
1	10/26/2015	12345	Voyager	IBM	1,000	139.02	139,020
2	10/26/2015	12345	Voyager	AMGN	500	158.94	79,470
3	10/26/2015	12345	Voyager	AAPL	2,000	118.27	236,540
4	10/26/2015	987654	Ping	WMT	4,000	57.48	229,920
5	10/26/2015	987654	Ping	KO	8,000	42.34	338,720
6	10/27/2015	12345	Voyager	IBM	1,000	140.01	140,010
7	10/27/2015	12345	Voyager	AMGN	500	158.94	79,470
8	10/27/2015	12345	Voyager	AAPL	2,000	118.27	236,540
9	10/27/2015	987654	Ping	WMT	4,500	57.48	258,660
10	10/27/2015	987654	Ping	KO	8,000	42.34	338,720
11	10/28/2015	12345	Voyager	IBM	1,000	139.02	139,020
12	10/28/2015	12345	Voyager	AMGN	600	159.55	95,730
13	10/28/2015	12345	Voyager	AAPL	1,000	117.55	117,550
14	10/28/2015	987654	Ping	WMT	5,000	57.48	287,400
15	10/28/2015	987654	Ping	KO	8,000	41.21	329,680
16	10/29/2015	12345	Voyager	IBM	2,000	139.02	278,040
17	10/29/2015	12345	Voyager	AMGN	600	158.94	95,364
18	10/29/2015	12345	Voyager	AAPL	1,000	118.27	118,270
19	10/29/2015	987654	Ping	WMT	6,000	57.48	344,880
20	10/29/2015	987654	Ping	KO	9,000	42.34	381,060
21	10/30/2015	12345	Voyager	IBM	2,000	139.02	278,040
22	10/30/2015	12345	Voyager	AMGN	700	159.99	111,993
23	10/30/2015	12345	Voyager	AAPL	1,000	117.49	117,490
24	10/30/2015	987654	Ping	WMT	5,000	57.22	286,100
25	10/30/2015	987654	Ping	KO	10,000	40.24	402,400

Figure 4-13. Historical portfolio holdings data volume (large format, color version (https://oreil.ly/dqef-4-13))

The model uses the control values illustrated in Figure 4-14 to validate the number of records and the market value of the raw portfolio holdings data illustrated in Figure 4-15. The control values are provided by the accounting platform in a separate data file and are used to validate the raw portfolio holdings data.

Processing	Account	Record Count	Market Value
11/2/2015	12345	3	453,995
11/2/2015	987654	2	545,560

Figure 4-14. Portfolio holdings control data

Record	Processing Date	Account	Ticker	Quantity	Bid	Market Value
1	11/2/2015	12345	IBM	920	139.02	127,898
2	11/2/2015	12345	AMGN	500	159.99	79,995
3	11/2/2015	12345	AAPL	2,000	117.49	234,980
4	11/2/2015	987654	WMT	4,000	57.29	229,160

Figure 4-15. Raw portfolio holdings data

The model applies the collection DQS to the uncleansed, raw portfolio holdings data illustrated in Figure 4-15. The collection DQS are the same for each downstream business function and are defined for the portfolio holdings data in this model. Table 4-17 outlines the data quality tolerances for the portfolio holdings data volume. The model uses valid and invalid tolerances; however, you could add one or more suspect tolerances or other sophisticated logic if that is more appropriate for your data.

Table 4-17. Collection DQS

Data volume	Data quality description	DQS	Business impact
Portfolio holdings	All portfolio holding records and data elements are mandatory and must exist. Use completeness DQS.	Portfolio holdings: Collection —record count = V, Raw Record Count = control Record Count, IV, Raw Record Count ≠ control Record Count, H	High
	The account and portfolio holdings must be identifiable using the Account and Ticker. Use cohesion DQS.		
	The Record Count in the portfolio holdings control data must match the Record count in the raw portfolio holdings data volume to be valid; otherwise it is invalid, and the business impact is high.	Portfolio holdings: Collection —market value Percent Difference = V, Raw Market Value < 3% control Market Value, IV, Raw Market Value ≥ 3% control Market Value, H	High
	The percentage difference between the sum of the Market Values of the raw portfolio holdings data for an account must be less than 3% of the official Market Value of the portfolio in the portfolio holdings control data to be valid; otherwise, it is invalid, and the business impact is high.		

The collection DQS for the portfolio holdings indicate all records and data elements are mandatory and must exist, and the account and portfolio holdings must be identifiable. The application of completeness DQS and cohesion DQS have been intentionally omitted for brevity. The collection DQS require that the raw portfolio holdings Record count for each account equal the corresponding portfolio holdings control Record Count. This means if the record counts match, then the collection is valid; otherwise, if the record counts do not match, then the collection is invalid. In addition, the DQS requir that the difference between the raw portfolio holdings Market Value for each account and the corresponding control Market Value be less than 3% to be valid; otherwise, the collection is invalid.

Figure 4-16 illustrates the results and shows the valid or invalid Record Count data quality metric for each collection. Figure 4-16 includes a copy of the Raw Record Count datum values in the column titled "Raw Record Count2," for reference.

Account	Raw Record Count	Control Record Count	Raw Record Count2
12345	V	3	3
987654	IV	2	1

Figure 4-16. Collection record count data quality metrics (large format, color version (https://oreil.ly/dqef-4-16))

Figure 4-17 illustrates the results and shows the valid or invalid Market Value data quality metric for each collection. Figure 4-17 includes a copy of the Raw Market Value datum values in the column titled "Raw Market Value2," for reference. The difference between the raw Market Value and the control Market Value is expressed as a percentage for illustration purposes.

Account	Raw Market Value	Control Market Value	Raw Market Value2	Percent Difference
12345	V	453,995	442,873	2.5%
987654	IV	545,560	229,160	138.1%

Figure 4-17. Collection market value percent difference data quality metrics (large format, color version (https://oreil.ly/dqef-4-17))

Applying the DQS for the collection data dimension to the raw portfolio holdings data volume generates both statistics and data quality metrics. The statistics for the raw portfolio holdings data volume in Figures 4-16 and 4-17 are as follows:

- 4 datum records
- 2 data elements (Market Value and Record Count)
- 4 datum values

Table 4-18 shows the total number of valid and invalid datum values in the raw portfolio holdings data volume.

Table 4-18. Summary of collection data quality metrics

Data element	Valid	Invalid
Record Count	1	1
Market Value	1	1
Metrics totals	2	2

The collection data dimension is specific to the type of collection (e.g., portfolio holdings, ETF, index). A valid collection means all required records exist and are identifiable. A valid collection can contain invalid datum values, as long as the invalid datum is not required to validate the collection itself. Control totals, such as record counts and portfolio holdings market values, are useful to validate collections. However, if control totals are not available for use in the validation, then (as demonstrated with the market value tolerance), you can use a congruence prior value comparison or congruence z-score instead. The collection validation, like all other tolerance validations except accuracy, does not guarantee the data is valid and correct. Instead, as mentioned in Chapter 3, the collection validation check will identify anomalies.

Example

This is a simple example to illustrate the special nature of data collections and the mechanics of applying validation checks to confirm the validity of a collection. You are encouraged to develop your own collection validation checks and relevant data quality tolerances using more sophisticated logic that may be more applicable and useful to identify data anomalies relative to the nature of the data.

Let's say two datum values are within the valid tolerance. However, two data anomalies are identified using the collection data quality validation defined in the DQS. These two anomalies do not meet the valid tolerance condition. Control totals (such as market value for portfolio holdings, weights and total weights for indices and ETFs, and general record counts) are useful for detecting anomalies or outliers. While the Market Value percent difference for account 12345 is 2.5% and within our DQS valid tolerance, we also know that on 11/2/2015, 80 shares of Apple stock was sold yielding a quantity of 920 shares. The sale is reflected in the raw portfolio holdings Market Value, which is $442,873. However, the sale has not been reflected in the portfolio holdings control data Market Value, which is $453,995. The record counts clearly indicate a portfolio holding record is missing for account 987654 and the percent difference between the raw Market Value and the control Market Value of 138.1% is an outlier. It is unclear what has happened to the portfolio holdings for account 987654. The portfolio holding record may have been mistakenly omitted, or the holding may have been completely sold but not recorded. Since both the Record Count and the Market Value data elements are not within the expected valid tolerance, they require further inspection and review.

Cohesion DQS

As mentioned in Chapter 3, the cohesion data dimension refers to the relationship between datum values that are typically organized as logical records of data. Generally, all datum values have a relationship to some other datum. This means the datum values must be organized and, at a minimum, paired with some form of identifier that links one datum or set of datum values to another and facilitates joining two or more datasets using the identifier. The identifier is often referred to as a primary key or foreign key. The identifier may be one datum value or may be a combination of datum values. In either case, the objective is to establish a precise relationship that enables you to join data together.

The security master data volume illustrated in Figure 4-18 contains the Processing Date and the Ticker. Together, these two data elements uniquely identify the data record for a specific date. The record contains the Issue Name, Exchange, Bid, Ask, Spread, and so on.

The cleansed and validated historical portfolio holdings data volume illustrated in Figure 4-18 contains the Processing Date and Account as primary data keys. Together, these two data elements uniquely identify the data record for a specific date. The record contains the Account Name, Ticker, Quantity, Bid, and Market Value. The Ticker data element in the holdings data volume, along with the Processing Date data element, are referred to as foreign data keys. These keys link to the Processing Date data element and Ticker data element that are part of the primary data key in the security master data volume. The cohesion data dimension for this data volume is valid if this relationship exists and the foreign-key-to-primary-key relationship is valid.

You will use the completeness, conformity, and if possible, accuracy DQS to validate the primary and foreign data key elements. You will use the timeliness DQS to validate the date, time, or date-time if the data volume is a time series. The primary and foreign data keys are mandatory to uniquely identify the datum records and to enable cohesion in cross-data volume linkages. Figure 4-18 illustrates the primary data key and foreign data key relationship between the security master data volume and the portfolio holdings data volume.

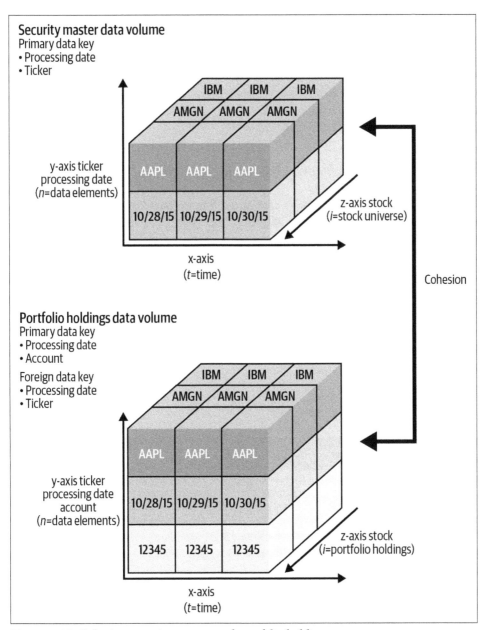

Figure 4-18. Cohesion security master and portfolio holdings

The model uses the raw portfolio holdings data illustrated in Figure 4-19.

Record	Processing Date	Account	Ticker	Quantity	Bid	Market Value
1	11/3/2015	12345	IBM	1,100	139.54	153,494
2	11/3/2015	12345	AMGN	700	160.05	112,035
3	11/3/2015	12345	DELL	1,900	118.67	225,473
4	11/3/2015	987654	WMT	3,500	57.98	202,930
5	11/3/2015	987654	KO	9,500	40.21	381,995

Figure 4-19. Unknown ticker raw portfolio holdings data volume

The Ticker is a mandatory field, as part of the foreign data key, to uniquely identify the portfolio holding record along with the Processing Date and Account. Applying the completeness, conformity, and accuracy DQS to the Ticker data element in the unknown ticker raw portfolio holdings data volume indicates all the Ticker datum values are valid. The model applies the cohesion DQS outlined in Table 4-19 to the unknown ticker raw portfolio holdings data volume. The cohesion DQS are the same for each downstream business function and are defined for the portfolio holdings data volume in this model. Table 4-19 outlines the data quality tolerances for the portfolio holdings data volume. The model assigns valid and invalid metrics by matching the foreign data key (Processing Date, Ticker) in the unknown ticker raw portfolio holdings data to the primary data key (Processing Date, Ticker) in the security master data volume.

Table 4-19. Cohesion DQS

Data volume	Data quality description	DQS	Business impact
Portfolio holdings	All portfolio holding records and data elements are mandatory and must exist. Use completeness DQS. The portfolio holdings stock Ticker for a specific Processing Date must match and link to the same stock Ticker and Processing Date in the security master data volume to be valid; otherwise it is invalid, and the business impact is high.	Portfolio holdings: Cohesion = V, raw holdings (Processing Date + Ticker) = security master (Processing Date + Ticker), IV, raw holdings (Processing Date + Ticker) ≠ security master (Processing Date + Ticker), H	High

When these primary and foreign data key relationships are well defined and enforced in physical data structures, such as databases, then the technology can enforce cohesion across data volumes using primary and foreign key relationships. However, the financial industry uses many diverse data volumes and technologies that have evolved over time. You may not be able to rely on the data management technology to enforce cohesion. Therefore, you may need to implement special cohesion data validations to ensure data volumes can be linked to one another.

The cohesion DQS for the raw portfolio holdings indicate the Processing Date and Ticker data elements are mandatory and must exist and the account and portfolio holdings must be identifiable. The Ticker and the Processing Date for each portfolio holding must match the Ticker and the Processing Date in the security master data volume. The application of completeness, conformity, accuracy, and cohesion DQS for the Account are valid and have been intentionally omitted for brevity. The cohesion DQS require the raw portfolio holdings Ticker and Processing Date match the Ticker and Processing Date for each portfolio holdings record in the security master data volume. This means if the foreign data key (Processing Date, Ticker) for each record in the raw portfolio holdings volume matches the primary data key (Processing Date, Ticker) in the security master data volume, then the cohesion of the data record is valid; otherwise, if the foreign data key and primary data key for each record do not match, then the cohesion of the data record is invalid.

Figure 4-20 illustrates the results and shows the valid or invalid portfolio holdings records using the Processing Date and Ticker data quality metrics. Figure 4-20 includes a copy of the Processing Date and Ticker datum values in columns titled "Processing Date2" and "Ticker2," for reference.

Record	Processing Date	Account	Ticker	Processing Date2	Ticker2
1	V	12345	V	11/3/2015	IBM
2	V	12345	V	11/3/2015	AMGN
3	IV	12345	IV	11/3/2015	DELL
4	V	987654	V	11/3/2015	WMT
5	V	987654	V	11/3/2015	KO

Figure 4-20. Cohesion data quality metrics (large format, color version (https://oreil.ly/ dqef-4-20))

The application of the DQS for the cohesion data dimension to the raw portfolio holdings data volume generates both statistics and data quality metrics. The statistics for the raw portfolio holdings data volume in Figure 4-20 are as follows:

- 5 datum records
- 2 data elements (Processing Date and Ticker)
- 10 datum values

Table 4-20 shows the total number of valid and invalid datum values in the raw portfolio holdings data volume.

Table 4-20. Summary of cohesion data quality metrics

Data element	Valid	Invalid
Processing Date	4	1
Ticker	4	1
Metrics totals	8	2

The cohesion data dimension reflects the ability of data volumes to be linked together. Cohesion between data volumes is specific to the nature of the data and the data elements, or combination of data elements, that constitute the primary data keys in one data volume and the foreign data keys in another data volume (e.g., Processing Date, Ticker). A volume of data with valid cohesion means the foreign data keys that identify records in one data volume match to the primary data keys that identify records in another data volume.

Any data volume can have valid cohesion and contain invalid datum values, as long as the invalid datum values are not those datum values required to validate the relationship to another data volume. The cohesion validation does not guarantee the data is valid and correct. Instead, as mentioned in Chapter 3, the validation check will identify anomalies.

Example

This is a simple example to illustrate the relationship, or cohesion, between data volumes and the mechanics of applying validation checks to confirm the validity of the relationship. I encourage you to develop your own cohesion validation checks and relevant data quality tolerances using more sophisticated logic that may be more applicable and useful to identify data anomalies relative to the nature of the data.

Four foreign data key values (Processing Date, Ticker) in the raw portfolio holdings are within the valid tolerance. However, one foreign data key anomaly is identified using the cohesion data quality validation—it does not meet the valid tolerance condition. The raw portfolio holdings data volume contains a record with processing date 11/3/2015 and ticker DELL, but this Ticker does not exist in the security master data volume. It is unclear why the DELL stock security for account 12345 is in the raw portfolio holdings volume when there is no record of the DELL stock security in the security master data volume. The portfolio holdings for account 12345 and the security master maintenance process both require further inspection and review.

A summary of the data quality metrics is illustrated in Figure 4-21 after the holdings data volume as well as the securities, fundamentals, consensus recommendations, and prices data volumes have been corrected. Figure 4-21 illustrates the data quality status for the holdings, securities, fundamentals, consensus recommendations, and prices data volumes have changed from IV (invalid) to V (valid) or S (suspect). The quality of these data volumes now meets the DQS for all downstream consumers.

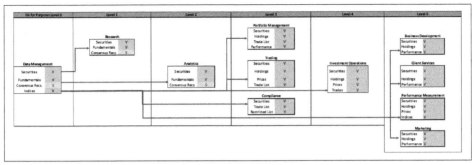

Figure 4-21. DQS model, including securities, fundamentals, consensus recommendations, prices, and holdings (large format, color version (https://oreil.ly/dqef-4-21))

Fit for Purpose

Fit for purpose means the quality of the data volumes required by business functions, applications, and data consumers satisfies the DQS for the function, application, and consumer. The DQS for each data dimension presented in this example are generally the same for all business functions and consumers. However, this is generally not the case in the real world. Data quality and DQS are highly specific to the data requirements of the business function, application, and data consumer. It is possible the DQS for data dimensions for one business function can be different than the DQS for a different business function.

For example, researchers, data scientists, and data analysts who explore and test new datasets that have not been integrated into the production data management pipelines may have lower data quality tolerances than other, more critical data volumes used in production pipelines.

The model in Figure 4-21 illustrates six levels of fit-for-purpose. You will want to think about the data processes in your business function, and the various business functions in your firm, with the defined business impacts in mind. The delineation of different fit-for-purpose levels in this model is for illustration purposes; however, the business impact definitions are highly applicable to all data processes and business functions. You may have more or less fit-for-purpose levels based on different DQS, but there will almost always be some level of negative business impact from the use of poor-quality data (or, data that is not fit-for-purpose). Table 4-21 outlines the fit-for-purpose levels for the business functions in this model. It also indicates the required data quality level and business impact of poor-quality data for each business function.

Table 4-21. Business impact and fit for purpose

Fit-for-purpose level	Business function(s)	Required data quality level	Business impact
0	Data Management	Low	None
1	Research	Medium	Waste high-value resources, time
2	Analytics	Medium	Waste high-value resources, time Poor analytics
3	Portfolio Management, Trading, Compliance	High	Damage at the financial, client regulatory, reputation levels
4	Investment Operations	High	Damage at the financial, client regulatory, reputation levels
5	Business Development, Client Services, Marketing, Performance Measurement	High	Damage at the financial, client regulatory, reputation levels

Level 0 is the lowest fit-for-purpose level and represents the initial raw vendor data ingestion commonly managed by a data management, data stewardship, or enterprise data management function. At this level, the data is raw and uncleansed, and the function applies various DQS to the data to validate its quality relative to the DQS of the downstream consumers.

Levels 1 and 2 represent the fit-for-purpose levels based on DQS and acceptable data quality levels for the Research business function and the use of data volumes for generating internal analytics. The required data quality level is medium, which means the business function is operationally functional with lower quality data. However, the business impact is medium—the time of high-value resources is wasted and analytics may be inaccurate or of poor quality, but there is likely no financial, regulatory, or client impact. Medium-level business impact typically requires triage to identify the data anomalies and determine the remediation actions necessary to improve the data quality.

Levels 3, 4, and 5 represent the fit-for-purpose levels based on DQS and acceptable data quality levels for the Portfolio Management, Trading, Compliance, Investment Operations, Business Development, Client Services, Performance Measurement, and Marketing business functions. The required data quality level is high, which means the business function is in an operational failure state with lower quality data. The business impact of incomplete or inaccurate data can include financial penalties, loss of client trust, regulatory violations, and reputational damage. High-level business impact requires an immediate response to identify the data anomalies and determine the remediation actions necessary to improve the data quality.

Summary

The model and the examples used in this chapter are intentionally simple, as they are meant to demonstrate the mechanics and value of DQS in a firm's data consumption pipeline. Data dimensions such as completeness, precision, and conformity can be viewed as having more general applicability to data. Completeness is applicable to all data of all data types. Conformity is applicable to any datum that must match a specific format, and precision is primarily applicable to numbers. The congruence dimension is typically used to validate time series numbers, but may also be used to validate time series of alpha and alphanumeric data. Congruence validations and tolerances are specific to the nature of the data. Timeliness validations are also specific to the nature of the data and are typically used to validate the date, time, or date-time of time series data volumes. Cohesion is specific to the relationship between data volumes and is thus specific to the nature of the data. Collection is a special dimension for data volumes that must contain all member data components to be valid collections. Finally, accuracy is specific and often unique to the data under inspection.

The application of DQS to each of these data dimensions, from general to specific, is illustrated in Table 4-22.

Table 4-22. DQS application to data dimensions

DQS application	Dimension
Specific	Accuracy
↑	Collection
	Cohesion
	Congruence
	Timeliness
	Conformity
	Precision
General	Completeness

Congratulations! You now know a lot more about data dimensions and the tools needed to quantitatively measure the shape of your data using defined valid, suspect, and invalid tolerances in DQS. The application and use of the DQS framework generates large volumes of data quality metrics. The next chapter introduces data quality visualizations that you can use to map and chart your analytics. The purpose of these visualizations is to enable you to quickly understand the spectrum and density of valid, suspect, and invalid data in your data volumes. You should be particularly interested in the suspect and invalid data that do not satisfy the fit-for-purpose DQS of consumers and that require further inspection, investigation, and likely remediation.

CHAPTER 5

Data Quality Metrics and Visualization

This chapter demonstrates how to visualize the data quality metrics that were generated in Chapter 4, after applying the DQS framework to data volumes.

Data Quality Metrics

As discussed, data quality metrics are the results generated from data quality measurements, defined in DQS, that are applied to your data. In Chapter 4, we applied the completeness DQS to the raw security master data volume. The statistics from the completeness data validation are 25 datum records comprised of 11 data elements for a total of 275 datum values. This yields 248 valid, 22 invalid, and 5 suspect data quality metrics for the completeness dimension. The metrics for all DQS applied to all data elements in the raw security master data volume are summarized in Table 5-1.

Table 5-1. Summary of data quality metrics after application of all DQS to raw security master data volume

Dimension	Data element	Valid	Invalid	Suspect
Completeness	Ticker	22	3	0
	Issue Name	22	3	0
	Exchange	20	5	0
	Bid	23	2	0
	Ask	21	4	0
	Spread	25	0	0
	Market Cap	25	0	0
	Market Cap Scale	23	2	0
	Price to Earnings (PE)	22	3	0
	Consensus Recommendation	21	0	4
	Consensus Date	24	0	1

Dimension	Data element	Valid	Invalid	Suspect
Timeliness	Consensus Date	15	6	4
Accuracy	Ticker	16	9	0
	Issue Name	11	14	0
	Exchange	20	5	0
Precision	Bid	17	2	6
	Ask	17	4	4
	Spread	17	3	5
	PE	20	3	2
Conformity	Issue Name	19	6	0
	Market Cap Scale	22	3	0
	Consensus Recommendation	19	2	4
Metrics totals		441	79	30

The model generated 550 data quality metrics for the completeness, timeliness, accuracy, precision, and conformity data dimensions, after applying the DQS to the raw security master data volume. This is a simple example with a small volume of data. You will likely use much larger volumes of data, and the total number of data quality metrics that can be generated using DQS for your real-world use cases may be quite large. This is where visualization techniques can play an important role in recognizing and understanding which data do or do not satisfy data quality tolerances defined in DQS.

Remember the DQS framework provides you with the tools to validate and confirm whether the dimensions of a data volume are valid. However, one of the strengths of the DQS framework is to provide the tools to precisely identify data anomalies. Data anomalies are identified when the generated data quality metric is suspect or invalid.

Data Quality Visualization

Data quality visualizations are visual representations of data quality metrics in the form of charts, graphs, maps, or other visual formats. Data visualization is a broad and complex discipline. For more on data visualization techniques, consult *Fundamentals of Data Visualization* by Claus O. Wilke (O'Reilly).

The human brain processes images approximately 60,000 times faster than it does text. Therefore, humans can more quickly understand the quality of data by using certain visualizations of the data, such as heatmaps and three-dimensional charts. The visualizations presented in this chapter are intended to demonstrate visualizing large volumes of data quality metrics for the purpose of identifying data anomalies (suspect or invalid datum).

Refer back to Figure 4-3 for a summary of completeness data quality metrics. In this figure, the metrics of valid, invalid, and suspect are shown as a heatmap. Figure 5-1 is a similar visualization that illustrates the data quality metrics generated after all DQS have been applied to the raw security master data volume in the model. The valid data quality metric is illustrated with V and the cell is highlighted in green (light gray, for you print book folks). The invalid metric is illustrated with IV and the cell is highlighted in red (dark gray in print books). The suspect metric is illustrated with S and the cell is highlighted yellow (medium gray in print books).

Record	Processing Date	Ticker	Issue Name	Exchange	Bid	Ask	Spread	Market Cap	Market Cap Scale	PE	Consensus Recommendation	Consensus Date
1	10/26/2015	V	IV	V	V	V	S	V	V	V	V	V
2	10/26/2015	IV	IV	IV	S	S	S	V	V	V	V	V
3	10/26/2015	V	V	V	V	V	V	V	V	V	V	V
4	10/26/2015	IV	V	V	V	IV	IV	V	V	V	V	V
5	10/26/2015	IV	V	V	IV	S	S	V	V	V	V	V
6	10/27/2015	V	IV	V	V	S	S	V	V	V	V	IV
7	10/27/2015	IV	IV	IV	S	S	S	IV	IV	V	V	IV
8	10/27/2015	V	V	V	S	IV	IV	V	V	V	V	IV
9	10/27/2015	V	IV	V	V	V	V	V	V	V	V	IV
10	10/27/2015	V	V	V	S	S	S	IV	IV	IV	IV	IV
11	10/28/2015	IV	IV	V	V	V	S	V	V	V	V	S
12	10/28/2015	IV	IV	IV	V	V	S	V	V	V	V	V
13	10/28/2015	IV	IV	V	IV	IV	S	V	V	S	S	IV
14	10/28/2015	V	V	V	V	V	V	IV	V	S	V	V
15	10/28/2015	V	V	V	V	S	V	V	V	IV	V	V
16	10/28/2015	V	IV	V	V	V	S	V	V	V	V	S
17	10/29/2015	IV	IV	IV	S	S	S	IV	IV	V	V	V
18	10/29/2015	V	V	V	V	V	V	V	V	V	S	V
19	10/29/2015	IV	V	V	V	V	V	IV	V	S	V	V
20	10/29/2015	IV	IV	IV	V	V	V	V	V	IV	S	S
21	10/30/2015	V	IV	V	V	IV	IV	V	V	V	S	S
22	10/30/2015	V	V	V	S	V	V	V	V	V	V	V
23	10/30/2015	V	IV	V	V	V	S	IV	V	V	IV	V
24	10/30/2015	V	IV	V	V	V	V	V	V	V	V	V
25	10/30/2015	V	V	V	V	V	V	V	V	V	V	V

Figure 5-1. Summary raw security master data quality heatmap (large format, color version (https://oreil.ly/dqef-5-01))

This visual approach is like a stop light, where green (light gray) means valid and the dimensions of the datum satisfy the valid tolerances in the DQS. The valid data is fit for purpose and can be used by downstream consumers. Yellow (medium gray) means suspect or caution and the datum is approaching an out-of-tolerance condition. The data may or may not be fit for purpose for use by downstream consumers, and thus requires investigation. Red (dark gray) means invalid and the dimensions of the datum do not satisfy the valid or suspect tolerances in the DQS. The data is *not* fit for purpose for use by downstream consumers.

The data quality metrics generated from applying the DQS of the completeness, timeliness, accuracy, precision, and conformity dimensions are summarized in this visualization using a prioritization logic. A *prioritization logic* is something that should now be familiar to us. It is used to summarize the data quality metric for a given datum and for all DQS validation checks applied to that specific datum. The summary data quality metric IV (invalid) is represented if any metrics are invalid. The summary data quality metric is S (suspect) if there are no invalid metrics but there are metrics that are suspect. And the summary data quality metric is V (valid) if there are no invalid or suspect metrics, and there are only valid metrics. The heatmap in Figure 5-1 is the summary of 550 data quality metrics prioritized to illustrate invalid, suspect, and valid data, after the DQS have been applied to the raw security master data volume.

Refer back to Figure 4-1 for an illustration of the DQS model. Each business function (e.g., Research, Analytics) requires specific data volumes (e.g., Securities, Prices, Holdings) to properly operate. Each business function has defined DQS for each data volume. Figure 4-1 illustrates the data quality status of each data volume, according to the model DQS using the raw, uncleansed security master and portfolio holdings data volumes. You can observe that the data quality metric is IV (invalid) for each data volume for each business function.

If you recall from Chapter 4, the Data Management function used the cleansed data (see Figure 4-11) to remediate the Ticker and Exchange data anomalies. Figure 5-2 illustrates the data quality metrics after both the Ticker and Exchange datum values have been remediated. You can observe that the data quality metrics for Ticker and Exchange have changed to V (valid) and are highlighted in green (light gray).

Record	Processing Date	Ticker	Issue Name	Exchange	Bid	Ask	Spread	Market Cap	Market Cap Scale	PE	Consensus Recommendation	Consensus Date
1	10/26/2015	V	IV	V	V	V	S	V	V	V	V	V
2	10/26/2015	V	V	V	S	S	S	V	V	V	V	V
3	10/26/2015	V	V	V	V	V	V	V	V	V	V	V
4	10/26/2015	V	V	V	V	IV	IV	V	V	V	V	V
5	10/26/2015	V	V	V	IV	S	S	V	V	V	V	V
6	10/27/2015	V	IV	V	V	S	S	V	V	V	V	IV
7	10/27/2015	V	V	V	S	S	S	IV	IV	V	V	IV
8	10/27/2015	V	V	V	S	IV	IV	V	V	V	V	IV
9	10/27/2015	V	IV	V	V	V	V	V	V	V	V	IV
10	10/27/2015	V	V	V	S	S	S	IV	IV	IV	IV	IV
11	10/28/2015	V	IV	V	V	V	S	V	V	V	V	S
12	10/28/2015	V	V	V	V	V	S	V	V	V	V	V
13	10/28/2015	V	IV	V	IV	IV	S	V	V	S	S	IV
14	10/28/2015	V	V	V	V	V	V	IV	V	S	V	V
15	10/28/2015	V	V	V	V	S	V	V	V	IV	V	V
16	10/29/2015	V	IV	V	V	V	S	V	V	V	V	S
17	10/29/2015	V	IV	V	S	S	S	IV	IV	V	V	V
18	10/29/2015	V	V	V	V	V	V	V	V	V	S	V
19	10/29/2015	V	V	V	V	V	V	IV	V	S	V	V
20	10/29/2015	V	IV	V	V	V	V	V	V	IV	S	S
21	10/30/2015	V	IV	V	V	IV	IV	V	V	V	S	S
22	10/30/2015	V	V	V	S	V	V	V	V	V	V	V
23	10/30/2015	V	IV	V	V	V	S	IV	V	V	IV	V
24	10/30/2015	V	IV	V	V	V	V	V	V	V	V	V
25	10/30/2015	V	V	V	V	V	V	V	V	V	V	V

Figure 5-2. Summary cleansed security master data quality heatmap (Ticker and Exchange anomalies resolved) (large format, color version (https://oreil.ly/dqef-5-02))

The Data Management function remediates the Issue Name data anomalies. Figure 5-3 illustrates the data quality metrics after the Issue Name data has been corrected. You can observe the data quality metric for the Issue Name datum values has changed to V (valid) and are highlighted in green (light gray).

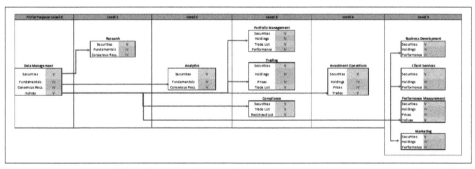

Processing Date	Ticker	Issue Name	Exchange	Bid	Ask	Spread	Market Cap	Market Cap Scale	PE	Consensus Recommendation	Consensus Date
10/26/2015	V	V	V	V	V	S	V	V	V	V	V
10/26/2015	V	V	V	S	S	S	V	V	V	V	V
10/26/2015	V	V	V	V	V	V	V	V	V	V	V
10/26/2015	V	V	V	V	IV	IV	V	V	V	V	V
10/26/2015	V	V	V	IV	S	S	V	V	V	V	V
10/27/2015	V	V	V	V	S	S	V	V	V	V	IV
10/27/2015	V	V	V	S	S	S	IV	IV	V	V	IV
10/27/2015	V	V	V	S	IV	IV	V	V	V	V	IV
10/27/2015	V	V	V	V	V	V	V	V	V	V	IV
10/27/2015	V	V	V	S	S	S	IV	IV	IV	IV	IV
10/28/2015	V	V	V	V	V	S	V	V	V	V	S
10/28/2015	V	V	V	V	V	S	V	V	V	V	V
10/28/2015	V	V	V	IV	IV	S	V	V	S	S	IV
10/28/2015	V	V	V	V	V	V	IV	V	V	S	V
10/28/2015	V	V	V	V	S	V	V	V	IV	V	V
10/29/2015	V	V	V	V	V	S	V	V	V	V	S
10/29/2015	V	V	V	S	S	S	IV	IV	V	V	V
10/29/2015	V	V	V	V	V	V	V	V	V	S	V
10/29/2015	V	V	V	V	V	V	IV	V	S	V	V
10/29/2015	V	V	V	V	V	V	V	V	IV	S	S
10/30/2015	V	V	V	V	IV	IV	V	V	V	S	S
10/30/2015	V	V	V	S	V	V	V	V	V	V	V
10/30/2015	V	V	V	V	V	S	IV	V	V	IV	V
10/30/2015	V	V	V	V	V	V	V	V	V	V	V
10/30/2015	V	V	V	V	V	V	V	V	V	V	V

Figure 5-3. Summary cleansed security master data quality heatmap (Issue Name anomalies resolved) (large format, color version (https://oreil.ly/dqef-5-03))

The summary data quality metrics are illustrated in Figure 5-4 after the data has been corrected. Figure 5-4 shows that the data quality status for the securities data volume (which includes Ticker, Issue Name, and Exchange datum values) has changed from IV (invalid) to V (valid) and is highlighted in green (light gray). Data in the securities data volume now satisfies the valid tolerances defined in the DQS for all downstream consumers.

Figure 5-4. DQS model with anomalies in the securities data volume resolved (large format, color version (https://oreil.ly/dqef-5-04))

The Data Management function remediates the Bid, Ask, and Spread data anomalies, and Figure 5-5 illustrates the resulting data quality metrics. You can observe that the data quality metrics for the Bid, Ask, and Spread datum values have changed to V (valid) and are highlighted in green (light gray).

Processing Date	Ticker	Issue Name	Exchange	Bid	Ask	Spread	Market Cap	Market Cap Scale	PE	Consensus Recommendation	Consensus Date
10/26/2015	V	V	V	V	V	V	V	V	V	V	V
10/26/2015	V	V	V	V	V	V	V	V	V	V	V
10/26/2015	V	V	V	V	V	V	V	V	V	V	V
10/26/2015	V	V	V	V	V	V	V	V	V	V	V
10/26/2015	V	V	V	V	V	V	V	V	V	V	V
10/27/2015	V	V	V	V	V	V	V	V	V	V	IV
10/27/2015	V	V	V	V	V	V	IV	IV	V	V	IV
10/27/2015	V	V	V	V	V	V	V	V	V	V	IV
10/27/2015	V	V	V	V	V	V	V	V	V	V	IV
10/27/2015	V	V	V	V	V	V	IV	IV	IV	IV	IV
10/28/2015	V	V	V	V	V	V	V	V	V	V	S
10/28/2015	V	V	V	V	V	V	V	V	V	V	V
10/28/2015	V	V	V	V	V	V	V	V	S	S	IV
10/28/2015	V	V	V	V	V	V	IV	V	S	V	V
10/28/2015	V	V	V	V	V	V	V	V	IV	V	V
10/29/2015	V	V	V	V	V	V	V	V	V	V	S
10/29/2015	V	V	V	V	V	V	IV	IV	V	V	V
10/29/2015	V	V	V	V	V	V	V	V	V	S	V
10/29/2015	V	V	V	V	V	V	IV	V	S	V	V
10/29/2015	V	V	V	V	V	V	V	V	IV	S	S
10/30/2015	V	V	V	V	V	V	V	V	V	S	S
10/30/2015	V	V	V	V	V	V	V	V	V	V	V
10/30/2015	V	V	V	V	V	V	IV	V	V	IV	V
10/30/2015	V	V	V	V	V	V	V	V	V	V	V
10/30/2015	V	V	V	V	V	V	V	V	V	V	V

Figure 5-5. Summary cleansed security master data quality heatmap (Bid, Ask, and Spread anomalies resolved) (large format, color version (https://oreil.ly/dqef-5-05))

The summary data quality metrics are illustrated in Figure 5-6 after the data has been corrected. Figure 5-6 shows that the data quality status for the prices data volume (which includes Bid, Ask, and Spread datum values) has changed from IV (invalid) to V (valid) and is highlighted in green (light gray). Data in the prices data volume now satisfies the valid tolerances defined in the DQS for all downstream consumers.

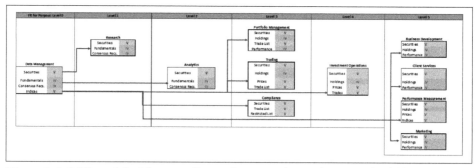

Figure 5-6. DQS model with anomalies in the prices data volume resolved (large format, color version (https://oreil.ly/dqef-5-06))

The Data Management function remediates the Market Cap, Market Cap Scale, and PE data anomalies. Figure 5-7 illustrates the resulting data quality metrics. You can see that the data quality metrics for the Market Cap, Market Cap Scale, and PE datum values have changed to V (valid) and are highlighted in green (light gray).

Processing Date	Ticker	Issue Name	Exchange	Bid	Ask	Spread	Market Cap	Market Cap Scale	PE	Consensus Recommendation	Consensus Date
10/26/2015	V	V	V	V	V	V	V	V	V	V	V
10/26/2015	V	V	V	V	V	V	V	V	V	V	V
10/26/2015	V	V	V	V	V	V	V	V	V	V	V
10/26/2015	V	V	V	V	V	V	V	V	V	V	V
10/26/2015	V	V	V	V	V	V	V	V	V	V	V
10/27/2015	V	V	V	V	V	V	V	V	V	V	IV
10/27/2015	V	V	V	V	V	V	V	V	V	V	IV
10/27/2015	V	V	V	V	V	V	V	V	V	V	IV
10/27/2015	V	V	V	V	V	V	V	V	V	V	IV
10/27/2015	V	V	V	V	V	V	V	V	V	IV	IV
10/28/2015	V	V	V	V	V	V	V	V	V	V	S
10/28/2015	V	V	V	V	V	V	V	V	V	V	V
10/28/2015	V	V	V	V	V	V	V	V	V	S	IV
10/28/2015	V	V	V	V	V	V	V	V	V	V	V
10/28/2015	V	V	V	V	V	V	V	V	V	V	V
10/29/2015	V	V	V	V	V	V	V	V	V	V	S
10/29/2015	V	V	V	V	V	V	V	V	V	V	V
10/29/2015	V	V	V	V	V	V	V	V	V	S	V
10/29/2015	V	V	V	V	V	V	V	V	V	V	V
10/29/2015	V	V	V	V	V	V	V	V	V	S	S
10/30/2015	V	V	V	V	V	V	V	V	V	S	S
10/30/2015	V	V	V	V	V	V	V	V	V	V	V
10/30/2015	V	V	V	V	V	V	V	V	V	IV	V
10/30/2015	V	V	V	V	V	V	V	V	V	V	V
10/30/2015	V	V	V	V	V	V	V	V	V	V	V

Figure 5-7. Summary cleansed security master data quality heatmap (Market Cap, Market Cap Scale, and PE anomalies resolved) (large format, color version (https://oreil.ly/dqef-5-07))

Figure 5-8 reveals that the data quality status for the fundamentals data volume (which includes Market Cap, Market Cap Scale, and PE datum values) has changed from IV (invalid) to V (valid) and is highlighted in green (light gray). The data in the fundamentals data volume now satisfies the valid tolerances defined in the DQS for all downstream consumers.

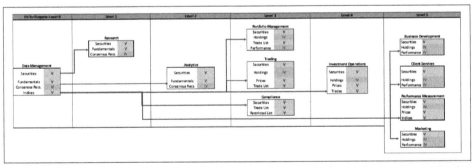

Figure 5-8. DQS model with anomalies in the fundamentals data volume now resolved (large format, color version (https://oreil.ly/dqef-5-08))

The Data Management function remediates the Consensus Recommendation and Consensus Date data anomalies, and Figure 5-9 illustrates the resulting data quality metrics after the consensus recommendation and consensus date data has been corrected. You can observe the data quality metrics for the Consensus Recommendation and Consensus Date datum values have changed to V (valid) and are highlighted in green (light gray).

Processing Date	Ticker	Issue Name	Exchange	Bid	Ask	Spread	Market Cap	Market Cap Scale	PE	Consensus Recommendation	Consensus Date
10/26/2015	V	V	V	V	V	V	V	V	V	V	V
10/26/2015	V	V	V	V	V	V	V	V	V	V	V
10/26/2015	V	V	V	V	V	V	V	V	V	V	V
10/26/2015	V	V	V	V	V	V	V	V	V	V	V
10/26/2015	V	V	V	V	V	V	V	V	V	V	V
10/27/2015	V	V	V	V	V	V	V	V	V	V	V
10/27/2015	V	V	V	V	V	V	V	V	V	V	V
10/27/2015	V	V	V	V	V	V	V	V	V	V	V
10/27/2015	V	V	V	V	V	V	V	V	V	V	V
10/28/2015	V	V	V	V	V	V	V	V	V	V	V
10/28/2015	V	V	V	V	V	V	V	V	V	V	V
10/28/2015	V	V	V	V	V	V	V	V	V	V	V
10/28/2015	V	V	V	V	V	V	V	V	V	V	V
10/28/2015	V	V	V	V	V	V	V	V	V	V	V
10/29/2015	V	V	V	V	V	V	V	V	V	V	V
10/29/2015	V	V	V	V	V	V	V	V	V	V	V
10/29/2015	V	V	V	V	V	V	V	V	V	V	V
10/29/2015	V	V	V	V	V	V	V	V	V	S	S
10/29/2015	V	V	V	V	V	V	V	V	V	V	V
10/30/2015	V	V	V	V	V	V	V	V	V	V	V
10/30/2015	V	V	V	V	V	V	V	V	V	V	V
10/30/2015	V	V	V	V	V	V	V	V	V	V	V
10/30/2015	V	V	V	V	V	V	V	V	V	V	V
10/30/2015	V	V	V	V	V	V	V	V	V	V	V

Figure 5-9. Summary cleansed security master data quality heatmap (Consensus Recommendation and Consensus Date anomalies resolved) (large format, color version (https://oreil.ly/dqef-5-09))

Figure 5-10 illustrates the data quality status for the consensus recs data volume (which includes Consensus Recommendation and Consensus Date datum values) has changed from IV (invalid) to V (valid). The data in the consensus recs data volume now satisfies the valid and suspect tolerances defined in the DQS for all downstream consumers.

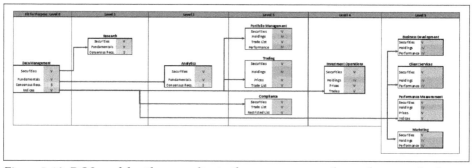

Figure 5-10. DQS model with anomalies in the consensus recs data volume resolved (large format, color version (https://oreil.ly/dqef-5-10))

The Data Management function remediates the holdings data anomalies, and Figure 5-11 shows the resulting data quality metrics after the holdings data is corrected. Performance data cannot be accurately generated until the holdings data has been remediated. Now that the holdings data is valid, the performance data is now valid. (Presentation of the detailed DQS and heatmap visualization for the holdings data has been intentionally omitted for brevity.) You can see that the data quality metric for the holdings data and performance data has changed to V (valid) and is highlighted in green (light gray).

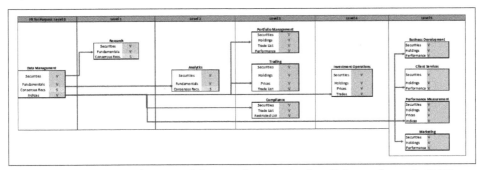

Figure 5-11. Summary of corrected data quality metrics for all data volumes in DQS model (large format, color version (https://oreil.ly/dqef-5-11))

The model demonstrates data quality engineering and, specifically, the application of DQS to data dimensions to do the following:

- Quantitatively measure dimensions
- Confirm that the data satisfies the valid tolerances defined in the DQS
- Identify the existence of any data anomalies

The model representation in Figure 5-11 illustrates that cleansed security master data volumes are provided to downstream consumers. These volumes satisfy the valid tolerances defined in the consumers' DQS. The data quality metrics heatmap visualizations allow users to quickly understand the valid, suspect, and invalid data quality metrics of data volumes.

Data quality metrics can also be charted. Figure 5-12 illustrates the data quality metrics in a three-dimensional bar chart. The valid data quality metrics are green (light gray), suspect metrics are yellow (medium gray), and invalid metrics are red (dark gray).

The purpose of the visualization of data quality metrics is to *quickly* identify anomalies. Therefore, if the charts include the valid data quality metrics, then the suspect and invalid metrics can be difficult to see.

Figure 5-13 omits the valid data quality metrics and illustrates only the suspect and invalid metrics.

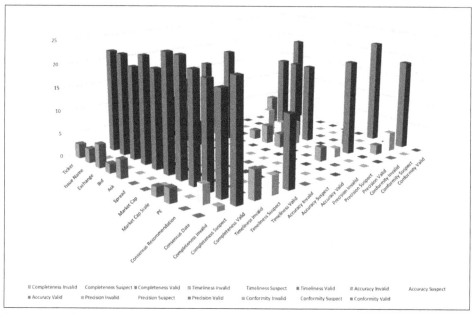

Figure 5-12. Summary raw security master data quality visualized as a bar chart (large format, color version (https://oreil.ly/dqef-5-12))

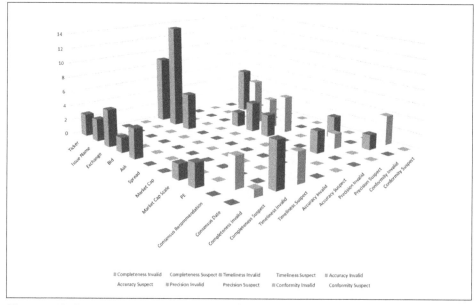

Figure 5-13. Summary raw security master data quality (suspect and invalid only) visualized as a bar chart (large format, color version (https://oreil.ly/dqef-5-13))

The chart in Figure 5-13 is more useful than the one in Figure 5-12 since you can quickly identify the suspect and invalid data quality metrics.

Conversely, the heatmap in Figure 5-9 illustrates the data quality metrics after all datum values in the security master data volume have been corrected. All but two data quality metrics are valid. There are two metrics that are suspect: Consensus Date and Consensus Recommendation. Figure 5-14 shows these valid and suspect data quality metrics.

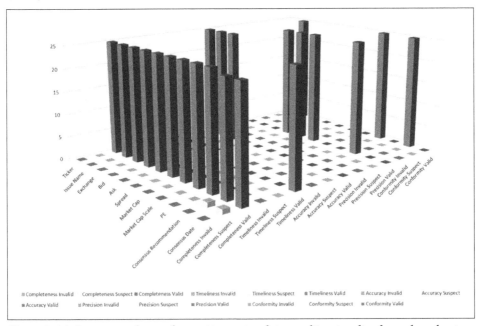

Figure 5-14. Summary cleansed security master data quality visualized as a bar chart (large format, color version (https://oreil.ly/dqef-5-14))

Summary

I hope you will design the visualizations of your data quality metrics so that you can quickly identify data anomalies. These visualizations are akin to those used in the data quality assurance processes in manufacturing, where physical properties of large volumes of raw materials are measured and evaluated relative to tolerances defined in control specifications. You are measuring dimensions of datum values in data volumes and evaluating those dimensions relative to tolerances defined in DQS. Use the resulting data quality metrics to identify data anomalies that require investigation and remediation, as well as to confirm that data volumes satisfy valid tolerances and are fit for purpose for use by consumers.

The next chapter details a sample operational efficiency cost model that demonstrates the value of pre-use data validations using the DQS framework. You will be able to use this model as a template and tailor the model inputs to align to your role, business function, or firm and illustrate similar cost efficiency opportunities using DQS and a pre-use data validation approach.

CHAPTER 6

Operational Efficiency Cost Model

This chapter presents a cost-based model that illustrates the cost of incorrect, out-of-tolerance data to a financial firm's operational efficiency. It is not a theoretical or subjective model, but rather a model that is based on the real costs of the employees' time that is spent and wasted when their work is affected by poor-quality data.

Demonstrating to your firm the benefits and impact of high-quality data can be challenging. We often hear stories about how data quality directly affects a firm's operation, and typically, these stories tend to be about negative events. Generally, you do not hear colleagues at the water cooler praising the quality of their data. Yet, you may hear something like, "I just spent half my day trying to figure out why the data was wrong."

The operational efficiency model we'll use in this chapter is designed to clearly demonstrate the cost of incorrect data in terms of employees' time and effort to work with and fix incorrect or misaligned data within a business function. The model also demonstrates the value of *accurate* data, which allows employees to spend their time efficiently instead of wasting their time triaging and solving data quality issues.

Model Details

This simple model is designed to demonstrate the cost of data, the cost of incorrect data, and the cost savings that can result from using pre-use data validations that employ the DQS framework versus post-use reconciliation techniques that are based on the cost of incorrect data as a function of the cost of those employees using the data. The annual cost of data is based on the cost of compensating employees.

The model illustrated in Table 6-1 reflects a manufacturing assembly line where the Data Management function ingests data (raw materials) at the beginning of the manufacturing line and more sophisticated, higher impact use of data typically occurs further down the assembly line (Trading, Compliance, and Client Reporting). The model does not include any other financial impact of the use of incorrect data. For example, the model does not illustrate the negative financial impact of incorrect trades, incorrect compliance, and client reporting, or misrepresentation of financial data to regulators. The financial and reputational cost of these types of events is highly subjective, but generally everyone agrees the business impact from these events can be severe. This model illustrates the business impact of incorrect data in terms of the cost of employees' time. You can expand, enhance, and adjust this model with more specific and precise details and more complex, real-world assumptions that reflect the business functions, data flows, number of data elements, and employee costs in your firm.

Model Cost Assumptions

The model outlined in Table 6-1 has several components, including the following:

Number of employees
  The number of employees in a business function

Average employee cost
  The cost of each employee in a business function that is assigned an average annual cost number, based on an average compensation cost

Operational efficiency expressed as business function cost
  The product of the average employee cost per business function multiplied by the number of employees in a business function

Number of data elements used by business function
  The number of unique data elements used within a business function

Cost per data element
  The operational efficiency expressed as business function cost divided by the number of data elements used by business function

Incorrect data cost
  The number of incorrect data elements multiplied by the cost per data element

The model assumes the following:

- The Data Management function distributes data volumes downstream to the Trading, Compliance, and Client Reporting business functions.

- The Data Management function performs data ingestion, structuring, data quality validation, and provisioning of data. This function employs lower cost resources compared to the other business functions.

- Downstream functions of Trading, Compliance, and Client Reporting have higher cost resources that are affected by incorrect data. Further, the impact of incorrect data on downstream business functions tends to have higher impact on the firm, such as incorrect data used for trading, failed compliance checks, or incorrect client and regulatory reporting. These can potentially lead to reputational risk, loss of business, and financial penalties.

- To maintain simplicity in the mechanics of the model, the same 20 incorrect data elements impact all business functions.

- A pre-use data validation percentage (0%, 50%, 70%, and 90%) is applied to operational efficiency expressed as business function cost. This percentage represents the portion of the cost of the employee's time that is saved since employees in downstream functions are spending less time tracking down data errors.

Table 6-1. Operational efficiency cost model (all numbers are annualized for simplicity)

Model component	Business function			
	Data Management	Trading	Compliance	Client Reporting
Number of employees	25	15	10	10
Average employee cost	$25,000	$30,000	$40,000	$75,000
Operational efficiency expressed as business function cost	$625,000	$450,000	$400,000	$750,000
Number of data elements used by business function	100	80	60	20
Cost per data element	$6,250	$5,625	$6,667	$37,500

Table 6-2 shows the cost impact of using traditional data reconciliation techniques, which means the data is not validated before being provided to the business function. Instead, the downstream business function receives and attempts to use the incorrect data and uses reconciliation techniques to validate the accuracy of the data. However, the business function is likely impaired due to the incorrect data, and the employees in the business function must spend time attempting to determine the cause of the incorrect data instead of doing their primary job tasks. This means the operational efficiency of the function is *negatively* impacted.

Table 6-2. Annual cost of incorrect data

Number of incorrect data elements	Annual cost of incorrect data (by business function)			
	Data Management	Trading	Compliance	Client Reporting
1	$6,250	$5,625	$6,667	$37,500
5	$31,250	$28,125	$33,333	$187,500
10	$62,500	$56,250	$66,667	$375,000
20	$125,000	$112,500	$133,333	$750,000
30	$187,500	$168,750	$200,000	$1,125,000
40	$250,000	$225,000	$266,667	$1,500,000
50	$312,500	$281,250	$333,333	$1,875,000

The annual cost of incorrect data in Table 6-2 is calculated using the number of incorrect data elements multiplied by the cost per data element from Table 6-1.

Post-use reconciliation assumes that the incorrect data flows from one business function to the next. The impacted function receiving the incorrect data then reconciles the data and determines how to correct it. However, the impacted function has just spent time (cost) to perform data reconciliation, determine the nature of the incorrect data, determine the correct data, and then use the correct data.

For example, the cost of 20 incorrect data elements per day for one year impacting the Trading function is $112,500 using post-use data reconciliation. This is the cost of the employees' time in the Trading function to analyze and reconcile 20 data elements daily, to identify the incorrect data, and to acquire the correct data.

Conversely, if you integrate pre-use data validations, defined by downstream processes in DQS, and identify and remediate the incorrect data before the data is provisioned, then the cost impact of incorrect data to the downstream processes is less than the cost from using post-use reconciliation techniques.

The model assumes that pre-use data validations based on the DQS of downstream consumers are known by the upstream Data Management function. The incorrect data does not flow to downstream functions until the data quality meets the DQS of the downstream functions. The responsibility to provision the correct data, and the cost of any required data remediation, is borne by the upstream function. Table 6-3 shows the pre-use data validation percentage for each business function. The pre-use data validation percentage is used to calculate the percentage of cost saving, by business function, if data is validated daily by the upstream business function providing the data.

Table 6-3. Pre-use data validation percentage

	Business function			
	Data Management	Trading	Compliance	Client Reporting
Pre-use data validation percentage	0%	50%	70%	90%

Table 6-4 shows the reduction in cost or operational efficiency of incorrect data in Trading, Compliance, and Client Reporting business functions using pre-use data validations. There is no benefit to operational efficiency for the Data Management function, since this is the first business function to ingest, validate, and provision the data. However, since ingestion, validation, and provisioning of data is the primary purpose of the Data Management function, then it is using its full operational efficiency to perform the data validation and remediation activities to meet the DQS of downstream consumers.

Table 6-4. Remaining cost of incorrect data after pre-use data validations

Number of incorrect data elements	Annual remaining cost of incorrect data elements after pre-use data validations (by business function)			
	Data management 0% pre-use validation, 100% remaining cost	Trading 50% pre-use validation, 50% remaining cost	Compliance 70% pre-use validation, 30% remaining cost	Client reporting 90% pre-use validation, 10% remaining cost
1	$6,250	$2,813	$2,000	$3,750
5	$31,250	$14,063	$10,000	$18,750
10	$62,500	$28,125	$20,001	$37,500
20	$125,000	$56,250	$40,002	$75,000
30	$187,500	$84,375	$60,003	$112,500
40	$250,000	$112,500	$80,004	$150,000
50	$312,500	$140,625	$100,005	$187,500

For example, the cost of 20 incorrect data elements per day for one year for the Trading business function using post-use reconciliation is $112,500 (Table 6-2). The pre-use data validation percentage for the Trading function is 50% (Table 6-3) and represents the model assumption that 50% of the incorrect data is identified and remediated by the Data Management function daily. Thus, the remaining cost of incorrect data for the Trading function is reduced by half. The cost of 20 incorrect data elements per day for one year for the Trading function using pre-use data validations defined in the DQS is $56,250 (Table 6-4). The use of pre-use data validation has a lower impact on the operational efficiency of the Trading function versus higher impact using post-use reconciliation.

Pre-use data validations based on the DQS of the downstream consumer or application are intended to reduce and minimize the cost or impact of incorrect data flowing downstream—like raw and semifinished materials flowing through a manufacturing assembly line. Data quality is verified upstream, according to the downstream functions' DQS, *before* the data is provided to the downstream process.

Conversely, *reconciliation* usually refers to performing data quality inspections *after* the data is received by the consuming system. It is often employed when data is expected to be used or after the application or consumer attempts to use the data, thus creating data errors that need to be researched. Meanwhile, the incorrect data is now already in the data ecosystems used by one or more business functions and applications. When the data is confirmed to be incorrect or malformed, it means multiple functions must waste time performing data cleanup efforts, re-sourcing the correct data, or overriding the incorrect data. This is politely called a *data mess* and it drains and damages operational efficiency.

Reconciliation Illustration

Question: What did the cow eat?

Reconciliation: Collect cow manure and compare the results from the cow's manure analysis to the approved dietary specification values to determine what the cow ingested.

Pre-use validation: Only feed the cow approved organic grass, vitamins, and water based on the cow's approved dietary specification. The inputs are known, controlled, measured, and verified. This is a primary quality control.

Conclusion: It is better and more pleasant to operate at the north end of the cow and control the inputs than at the south end of the cow. Results from a manure analysis can still be useful as a secondary, confirmation quality control. Gloves are recommended.

Reconciliation is a commonly used technique for identifying data anomalies and incorrect data in data volumes. Unfortunately, if this technique is used as the *primary* control for data quality validation and is employed at the time of a consumer's use—or worse, after attempted use—then the damage is already done. This results in wasted time, effort, and resources and, if not identified and corrected, potentially leads to incorrect data being used by other functions and critical processes.

The reconciliation technique can be an effective secondary data quality control that confirms and verifies data alignment and data quality post-use. Reconciliation should *not* be used as a primary data quality control. DQS and pre-use data validations should be used as primary controls.

Auditors and regulators tend to have more favorable, positive opinions about the robustness of an operational control framework if more than one control is actively used. If you use pre-use data validations as a primary control and reconciliation as a secondary verification control, then this control framework is more likely to meet audit and regulatory control standards.

Pre-Use Data Validations Versus Reconciliation

Table 6-5 shows the annual cost saved by downstream business functions when pre-use data validation is used versus reconciliation. The model assumes that pre-use data validation percentages of 50%, 70%, and 90% are applied daily to data used in the Trading, Compliance, and Client Reporting functions, respectively.

For example, the Trading function uses 80 data elements, of which 20 are incorrect. The cost of 20 data elements in terms of the Trading function's employee time is the cost per data element ($5,625) multiplied by the number of incorrect data elements (20), yielding $112,500. This means $112,500 of the annual operational efficiency of the Trading function is deducted and spent dealing with 20 incorrect data elements per day for one year.

If reconciliation is used by the Trading function, then the remaining cost impact for 20 incorrect data elements on the function's operational efficiency is the entire cost of $112,500. This means the incorrect data is used and fully impacts the Trading function. On the other hand, if pre-use data validations are used upstream by Data Management to remediate 50% of the incorrect data intended to be provisioned to the Trading function, then the remaining cost impact for 10 incorrect data elements on the function's operational efficiency is $56,250. Using pre-use data validations upstream has reduced the negative impact to the Trading operational efficiency, since employees are spending less time on fewer incorrect data elements. Therefore, the Trading function's operational efficiency benefits by saving $56,250, or 50% of the cost of incorrect data in terms of the employees' time that would have been wasted tracking down data errors for all the incorrect data elements.

If reconciliation is used by the Compliance function, then the remaining cost impact for 20 incorrect data elements on the function's operational efficiency is the entire cost of $133,340. This means the incorrect data is used and fully impacts the Compliance function. If pre-use data validations are used upstream by Data Management to remediate 70% of the incorrect data intended to be provisioned to the Compliance function, then the remaining cost impact for 6 incorrect data elements on the function's operational efficiency is $40,002. Here again, using pre-use data validations upstream has reduced the negative impact to the Compliance function's operational efficiency since employees are spending less time on fewer incorrect data elements. Therefore, the Compliance function's operational efficiency benefits by saving

$93,338 or 70% of the cost of incorrect data in terms of the employees' time that would have been wasted tracking down data errors for all the incorrect data elements.

If reconciliation is used by the Client Reporting function, then the remaining cost impact for 20 incorrect data elements on the function's operational efficiency is the entire cost of $750,000, since the function only uses 20 data elements and all 20 are assumed to be incorrect. This means the incorrect data is used and fully impacts the Client Reporting function. If pre-use data validations are used upstream by Data Management to remediate 90% of the incorrect data intended to be provisioned to the Client Reporting function, then the remaining cost impact for 2 incorrect data elements on the function's operational efficiency is $75,000. Using pre-use data validations upstream has reduced the negative impact to the Client Reporting function's operational efficiency since employees are spending less time on fewer incorrect data elements. Therefore, the Client Reporting function's operational efficiency benefits by saving $675,000 or 90% of the cost of incorrect data in terms of the employees' time that would have been wasted tracking down data errors for all the incorrect data elements.

This model demonstrates operational efficiency using the cost of employee compensation. However, recall from Chapter 4 and specifically Table 4-21, that the business impact and cost of incorrect data being used by Trading, Compliance, and Client Reporting can lead to misrepresentation to auditors, regulators, and clients. This will likely result in *severe*, negative business impact. The DQS framework empowers you to minimize these risks. The cost of regulatory penalties, loss of clients, and reputational damage is generally incalculable. Thus, the best course of action is *prevention*.

Table 6-5 shows that cumulative pre-use operational efficiency savings is $224,588. This is the total cost of all employee time saved by prevalidating a percentage of 20 incorrect data elements for each downstream business function before the data is provisioned to the functions. The lower cost is due to employees in downstream functions spending more time doing their job with correct data and less time wasted tracking down data errors for fewer incorrect data elements.

The total operational efficiency for all business functions is $2,225,000 (sum of top row of Table 6-5). This model demonstrates that post-use reconciliation reduces the operational efficiency by $995,840, which is the cost of the time wasted by employees using reconciliation techniques in downstream functions that are dealing with incorrect data. The model also demonstrates that the use of pre-use data validations does not entirely prevent all incorrect data from affecting downstream functions, but it reduces and attempts to minimize the negative impact to operational efficiency. Operational efficiency is still reduced by $771,252 even with the application of pre-use data validations. However, the overall operational efficiency benefits from

$224,588 in cumulative savings that would otherwise be wasted dealing with the full impact of incorrect data in each function.

Table 6-5. Summary annual cost comparison of 20 incorrect data elements

	Data management		Trading		Compliance		Client reporting	
	Post-use recon.	0% pre-use validated	Post-use recon.	50% pre-use validated	Post-use recon.	70% pre-use validated	Post-use recon.	90% pre-use validated
Operational efficiency expressed as business function cost	$625,000		$450,000		$400,000		$750,000	
Incorrect data elements	20		20		20		20	
Cost per data element	$6,250		$5,625		$6,667		$37,500	
Cost for 20 incorrect data elements	$125,000		$112,500		$133,340		$750,000	
Remaining cost impact for incorrect data elements	$125,000		$112,500	$56,250	$133,340	$40,002	$750,000	$675,000
Pre-use validation cost savings	N/A		N/A	$56,250	N/A	$93,338	N/A	$75,000
Impact of incorrect data on operational efficiency	$500,000		$337,500	$393,750	$266,667	$359,998	$0	$675,000
Cumulative pre-use operational efficiency savings	$0		N/A	$56,250	N/A	$149,588	N/A	$224,588

Summary

This chapter introduced a simple operational efficiency cost model that illustrates the cost difference between using post-use data reconciliation versus pre-use data validations based on DQS. Pre-use data validations intend to reduce and minimize the cost from incorrect data flowing downstream. Data quality is verified upstream, according to the downstream business function DQS, before the data is provided to the downstream function. Reconciliation is not recommended as a primary data quality control. Use pre-use data validations as primary controls and convert post-use data reconciliations into data verifications as secondary, confirming data quality controls.

This approach minimizes the impact and cost of incorrect data on downstream functions. You are encouraged to use this model as a template. Define and design more sophisticated, detailed, real-world model inputs and assumptions. Outline your business functions. Determine the cost of data used in functions, the impact of pre-use versus post-use data quality controls, and the cost differential between them for your business functions.

You now have a deeper understanding of the impact poor-quality data can have on the operational efficiency of your business functions. There are limitless approaches to quantifying the cost of incorrect data. The simple model in this chapter uses the cost of employees' time in terms of their compensation as a basis to calculate the cost of incorrect data elements. It is hard to argue with the cost side of the equation—everyone seems to have a natural appreciation for the relationship between maximizing their time and wasting it dealing with incorrect data.

The next chapter focuses on data governance and defining and curating data as an asset in your business function, or broadly across your organization. Data is very expensive, and the use of incorrect data is also very expensive. Thus, high-quality data is a very valuable asset and requires proper care and handling. You will see how the data governance function aligns with data quality and drives best practices for data definition, data architecture, and data management to deliver the highest quality data that is fit for purpose for your organization.

CHAPTER 7

Data Governance

This chapter introduces the primary components of data governance and provides program guidance and framework examples to help you implement a data governance initiative. The content will enable you to use the frameworks as a starting point—you will need to adjust and amend the program to your organization's culture and important data-oriented business objectives. Consult *Data Governance: The Definitive Guide* by Evren Eryurek et al. (O'Reilly) for detailed and comprehensive coverage of data governance.

This chapter is intended to provide basic data governance awareness and foundational concepts that will help you understand the role data governance plays in data quality engineering.

Do any of the following data issues sound familiar?

- Bad data is feeding applications.
- Inaccurate analytics, trade failures, and cash flow errors.
- Too many databases and data sources, prompting questions such as: Which should we use? Where is the right data? Where is our data inventory? Where did this data come from?
- Inconsistent data is presented to clients.
- Which data is approved for your use? When is the right data ready for you to use?
- Historical data does not link together over time.
- Development environments contain data that is easier to use, even though it is stale. You need the data, so you guess it is good enough.

- The number looks too high, too low, or wrong. You need to manually investigate, research, and verify.

- Are you getting good data from vendors? You pay a lot for it, so you should know.

- Your business function depends on data from a different function. How can you improve cross-function data alignment and efficiency?

These statements about data issues and questions about the location, integrity, and quality of data are all too familiar in the financial industry. Imagine if manufacturing professionals had similar questions and challenges about raw materials and their quality, where materials are located, or when they will be ready for the next step in the process. It is highly unlikely any reasonably sophisticated product would ever be produced. Further, high-quality, industrial manufacturing of complex pharmaceuticals, technical devices, communication networks, and smartphones, to name a few, would be impossible.

There are many variations of the definition of *data governance*. I define it as follows:

> *Data governance* refers to the comprehensive and disciplined management of data and its definition, relationships, availability, stewardship, ownership, quality, fitness for usability, integrity and veracity, and security.

Establishing a Data Governance Function

A robust data governance program typically includes an established Data Governance function that may be centralized, decentralized, or organizationally hybrid. The function promotes policies, processes, and procedures for governing data. It also promotes efficient operational execution and implementation of data governance processes in data processing and data-intensive projects.

Initiating a data governance program often begins with defining the owners, stewards, and custodians of the data assets in the enterprise. Such a program promotes the development and implementation of data governance policies that specify who has authority over the data and who is accountable for various aspects of it, including its quality validations, accuracy, accessibility, consistency, completeness, and maintenance.

A good program also proactively seeks to define and drive processes and procedures to effectively store, archive, and back up data. Further, given heightened cybersecurity concerns, governance programs require expert attention to data protection to minimize data breaches, accidental corruption, theft, or attack. Authorized personnel gain access to and use the data according to standards and procedures developed by the program. Data security and protection is often a joint effort between the data governance and the information security functions. Finally, rigorous and well-defined data management controls and audit procedures must be implemented to ensure ongoing compliance with existing, updated, or new regulations and laws.

The Data Governance function and the program implementation are collaborative endeavors, with the goal of embedding and institutionalizing changes in a firm's data management and usage practices. Data governance programs seek to evolve the stewardship of information assets according to defined policies, standards, and quality measurements. In this way, they support enhanced client service, optimize performance, reduce risk, and increase operational efficiency. The Data Governance function is typically a group of data experts and practitioners who drive the data governance program activities, monitor the data management operation, and define best practices and policies for data and its standard of care.

The key objectives of data governance are to ensure that data is understood, that data quality is measured and verified, and that data is certified as ready for use by the business.

Principles of Data Governance

General principles of a data governance program include the following:

- Data and its value are understood at all levels of the firm.
- Data is designed and integrated fit for purpose for a function.
- Data quality is defined, quantified, measured, and benchmarked.
- Data quality metrics and score-carding informs business and management decisions.
- Data usage and stewardship is organized with clear roles and responsibilities.
- Data governance is intended to enable the firm to maximize the value of its information assets to achieve greater performance and enhanced client service.

Data Governance Function

The Data Governance function supports and promotes an organization's detailed understanding of the data requirements necessary for effective business and technical operations. For example, the function seeks to establish defined stewardship and ownership roles that contribute to a clear understanding of who is responsible for the data and in what capacity. The function also tends to drive the implementation of business data dictionaries, logical data models, and defined data taxonomies and ontologies. These artifacts contribute to a firm's understanding of its data inventory. A Data Governance function is highly focused on understanding and defining the critical data quality requirements for provisioning high-quality data to consumers and applications.

What is the difference between data governance and data management?

- Data governance is the framework for establishing strategy, objectives, and policies for data management.

- Data management is the development and execution of architectures, practices, and procedures that *implement* data governance policies.

Table 7-1 outlines the general distinction between a Data Governance function and a Data Management function.

Table 7-1. Data Governance versus Data Management functions

Data Governance function	Data Management function
• Establishes the data governance operating model with defined policies, standards, procedures, and controls required to manage data • Provides oversight of the Data Management function, ensuring the data is managed according to the data governance policies • Monitors data quality using metrics generated by the Data Management function according to DQS • Monitors adherence to data management policies and standards	• Executes data management and control operations • Comprised of data stewards responsible for data quality and data provisioning • Manages data according to data governance policies and data management procedures • Generates data statistics and quality metrics based on DQS defined by data consumers

Data Governance Models

A Data Governance function can be implemented and positioned centrally, distributed across business units, or set up via a hybrid model—with centralized guidance and authority balanced with distributed functional authority. Table 7-2 lists the general organizational structure of a Data Governance function relative to firm size, management culture, and unique data governance requirements of the business functions.

Table 7-2. Data governance organizational models

Model	Description	Organizational alignment
Centralized	Single Data Governance function for policy, control guidance, and decision-making authority.	Tends to work well in hierarchical and large organizations with well-defined organizational structures and communications.
Distributed	Multiple Data Governance functions across the business, each with equal policy, control guidance, and decision-making authority.	Tends to work well in organizations with highly autonomous business functions and where business functions have unique data governance requirements.

Model	Description	Organizational alignment
Hybrid	Centralized data governance policy, control guidance, and certain decision-making authority.	Tends to work well in collaborative organizations using a hybrid model with centralized governance expertise and enterprise-level policy and decision making.
	Data governance units in each business function have localized decision-making authority.	Business unit governance functions implement enterprise policy while decision making is localized to the business function.

There are many factors to consider when selecting a data governance model that is expected to be effective and synergistic with an organization's existing structure and processes.

The following are key considerations when deciding on a governance model:

- Organizational change can be driven from the top, from the bottom (within functions), or by a hybrid combination.
- Policy development can be centralized, decentralized, or hybrid.
- Process alignment and change can be driven via a change management function or organically designed and implemented (i.e., it is decentralized).
- Definition, implementation, and access to physical data structures and applications can be managed centrally, distributed, or hybrid.
- Consider your firm's ability to successfully adopt and implement change while balancing other important, yet competing, business priorities.

Implementations of Data Governance functions are more successful when you align the function to your firm's operating culture and focus the function on delivering value to the business.

Creating a Data Governance Program

A data governance program often begins with collaborative engagement, leading to the establishment of a Data Governance function. Once established, the Data Governance function then serves as a center of excellence and provides policy, process, and metrics guidance across all aspects of data management for the firm.

Organizing the Program

A successful data governance program invites and includes key stakeholders from the most critical, data-intensive business functions across the firm. The general concept of data governance and the benefits of this function are not widely known in many organizations, so the program drives awareness and education to establish a working knowledge of data governance across the firm.

Collaborative engagement means engaging key stakeholders and integrating their feedback and contributions in the development of the data governance program. It involves the following:

- Establishing relationships with key stakeholders from various business functions, such as Investment Management, Research, Implementation, Trading, Operations, Information Technology (IT), and Compliance
- Outlining, developing, and socializing a data governance awareness program
- Establishing stakeholder buy-in and socializing the purpose of the program
- Determining functional team representatives, resources, program structure, methodology, and tools
- Organizing the data governance engagement model with senior leadership, functional management, and operational teams
- Documenting data management challenges, pain points, and opportunities for improvements, as well as defining current and future states
- Synthesizing feedback, incorporating feedback into the data governance development plan, and then confirming deliverables
- Determining program resources, structure, methodology, tools, and program communications
- Developing and organizing the program's communication plan

Establishing the Data Governance Council

As we've mentioned, one of the first steps in establishing a data governance program is creating a data governance council that acts as the working body of key stakeholders. These individuals have the expertise and insight to drive improvements in data alignment, data quality, data usage, and data processing in their respective business functions. The council is involved in the following:

- Organizing the data governance council, determining senior executive and working group members, meeting regularly, and providing data governance program updates

- Providing insight, guidance, and recommendations for changes and operational realignment efforts in data management usage processes and data stewardship roles
- Organizing and launching program workstreams, including:
  - Mapping data elements and developing a data dictionary
  - Defining DQS, metrics, and key performance indicators (KPIs)
  - Defining data management standards and data usage policies
  - Defining data quality measurements and assessment methods
  - Developing data governance training and education materials
  - Developing organizational messaging and program promotion
- Defining program measurements, metrics, and progress reporting, including:
  - Qualitative organizational impact measures, such as positive influence, raising awareness, and increasing the firm's understanding of the value of data as an asset
  - Quantitative business value measurements that contribute to improved internal customer satisfaction, attracting and retaining customer assets, cost savings, risk reduction, and efficiency improvements
  - Operational data measures, such as key metrics compared to DQS, policies, and benchmarks
  - Develop current and future state roadmap and refine during development
- Providing ongoing periodic data governance training to the firm

Engaging the Data Management Function

The Data Management function works with the Data Governance function to inventory the data assets of the firm, determine which data is most critical, define RACI (Responsible, Accountable, Consulted, Informed) matrix for critical data and data workflows, contribute to the definition and generation of DQS, and drive improvements in data management architectures. The Data Management function typically has deep expertise and insight into the characteristics of the firm's data, data use cases, data quality requirements, and common data issues. The function, with guidance from Data Governance, performs the following:

- Inventory and documenting of data stores, data inventory, and topology
- Inventory and documenting of critical data functions and data elements
- Building, aligning, and confirming the organizational RACI matrix
- Defining and documenting DQS, metrics, and quality measurements for data used by each business function and application

- Developing the data quality scorecard using valid, suspect, and invalid metrics relative to data quality dimensions (i.e., completeness, timeliness, accuracy, precision, conformity, congruence, collection, and cohesion)
- Defining the fit-for-purpose score calculations
- Determining productivity gains and/or cost savings
- Collaborating with the IT function to drive changes in data management architecture, strategic initiatives, and near-term opportunities
- Defining and establishing data stewardship and ownership roles and quality accountability

Engaging Business Functions

Business functions work with the Data Governance function to define and develop policies governing the use, accountability, and ownership of data that is used or generated. The business function typically defines the quality standards that are incorporated in DQS. They also determine the information sensitivity classification of data (e.g., unrestricted, confidential, restricted), which is used to align information security and data access controls. Various business functions engage with the Data Governance function to do the following:

- Define and develop a data management policy framework
- Develop common policies for data accountability and ownership
- Align data governance and stewardship within organizational roles and responsibilities
- Establish data capture and validation standards, and align data policies with retention and archiving requirements
- Enhance information security and data privacy policies, and align data access and usage control framework

Enhanced Data Governance Operating Model

The *enhanced data governance operating model* refers to an established Data Governance function that collaboratively assesses the implications and impact of data usage, the impact of data issues, and best practices for integrating new data. The function uses measurements, metrics, and reporting to provide ongoing feedback and recommendations to business functions about improvements, enhancements, and adjustments to data management practices and data usage activities. In this model, we tend to see the following:

- The data governance community is active, collaborative, and engaged.
- Data stewards and data owners with ownership and accountability are defined.

- Data dictionaries and inventories of firm-approved data assets are established.
- Data governance and management dashboards are used for information sharing.
- Qualitative and quantitative data measures (e.g., data quality metrics compared to DQS, policies, and benchmarks) are actively used and periodically refined and enhanced.
- Data governance contributes to and informs business decisions (e.g., new financial products, investment strategies, data classes, client requirements).
- Performance metrics are refined and enhanced based on results from Data Governance program reviews.
- Client, management, and operational feedback is synthesized with industry data management advances, and best practices are used to improve the Data Governance program.

Benefits of a Data Governance Program

A Data Governance program can benefit an organization in the following ways:

- Enables the delivery of high-quality, fit-for-purpose, business-ready data.
- Improves confidence in the quality of the data, resulting in less questioning and redundant verification.
- Supports the ability to potentially deliver the highest client service and investment returns possible.
- Empowers teams to deliver accurate insight and investment guidance to clients.
- Demonstrates transparency in the data discipline, which deepens client trust.
- Increases operational efficiency by providing the right data for a specific function's use.
- Enables compliance with regulatory mandates and supports risk management.
- Reduces costs by reducing and/or eliminating redundant data processing and duplicative, misaligned data content.
- Embeds data stewardship with data stewards who support data discovery, data definition, processing, enrichment and distribution. They use measurements, metrics, and reporting to inform the firm about data processing and quality.
- Potentially increases profitability by increasing operational efficiency and effectiveness.
- Drives increased visibility and recognition of the value of the data and information assets.

Data Governance Program Activities and Deliverables

Establishing a robust data governance program is no small endeavor. In this section, you will see how an organization's data governance program works in partnership with its Data Management function and how it drives implementation and use of precise DQS.

 There is no one-size-fits-all data governance program. You must understand and evaluate your firm's unique data challenges and determine which benefits of a data governance initiative are appropriate for your firm. You will need to determine which benefits yield the highest return and value when applied in combination with other data management and architecture improvements. You will also need to consider which data governance initiatives will have the *highest potential of success* given your firm's ability, willingness, and tolerance to adopt and implement change.

A data governance program will produce artifacts that will be used to drive improvements in data management operations, deliver higher quality data, and institutionalize your firm's appreciation and understanding of the value of its data. Table 7-3 outlines high-level data governance program activities and deliverables.

Table 7-3. Data governance program activities and deliverables

Framework	High-level data governance program activities	Deliverables
Policies and standards	• Develop and implement data governance policies and standards at the firm level and business function levels through cross-function collaboration. • Define the business leaders who are accountable for the quality and security of critical data. • Document and clarify the responsibilities of the business data owners, data stewards, and dependent stakeholders.	• Data usage policies and standards • Data ownership matrix • Defined roles
Data quality specifications (DQS)	• Help define the DQS used by each data consumer for each business function. Define comprehensive data quality validations for data dimensions (completeness, timeliness, accuracy, precision, conformity, congruence, collection, and cohesion).	• DQS
Data quality metrics	• Define data quality validation standards, measurements, and metrics. • Define business readiness, fit-for-purpose requirements. • Define data quality business impact scores.	• Data quality metrics, measurements, and validations

Framework	High-level data governance program activities	Deliverables
Business process and application changes	• Reengineer technology architecture and applications to precisely identify data and provision the right data to support the business function. • Implement data-governance-driven business process and data application changes.	• Business process and procedure changes • Application and data flow enhancements
Data inventory	• Define the critical data assets in business applications and related data stores used within each function.	• Data dictionary and related metadata

Data Governance Business Value

Demonstrating how data governance programs deliver business value can be challenging. Quantitative measurements yield greater confidence in a firm's collective recognition of business value, versus qualitative opinions. For example, providing a data quality report that uses metrics to show the data being used by business functions is complete and accurate could be impactful. These metrics, combined with tracking the reduction of data errors affecting business production processes, demonstrate the value of data controls.

A data governance program should be implemented with the intent to deliver meaningful results in the form of improved governance and stewardship of data, improved operational efficiency, improved confidence in data quality, improved data alignment to business function use, and reduction in operational cost and risk.

Table 7-4 summarizes the key business drivers and the investments necessary to deliver the anticipated business value from a data governance program.

Table 7-4. Data governance drivers, investments, and business value

Driver	Investment	Business value
Increased confidence in the data	• Develop and implement data governance policies and standards, at the firm and business function levels, that encourage cross-function collaboration and drive behavioral change • Define DQS for data used by each consumer for each business function • Reengineer technology architecture and applications to provision the right data to support the business function	Improve confidence in the data by: • explicitly defining data quality measures to reduce "noise" • using approved data to drive production processes • reducing data inconsistencies • prioritizing data-driven technology projects to improve data provisioning Increase data quality and alignment, driving: • greater data precision and support for improved insight and guidance • increased confidence in analytics • improved data accuracy • improved data quality for analyses and reporting

Driver	Investment	Business value
Cost reduction	• Implement data governance-driven business process and data application changes	Increase operational efficiency and reduce cost by: • reducing or eliminating redundant data processing and duplicative, misaligned data • reducing wasted effort in finding, questioning, reconciling, and revalidating data • improving time to market (e.g., quickly build client reports, use analytics in decisions faster)
Knowledge of data inventory	• Define the data and systems inventory, critical data assets, and related applications used within each function	Improve understanding and use of data assets with: • data dictionary • metadata and data lineage • data access and security
Data governance controls	• Define and implement data provisioning status, data quality metrics, and data validation controls • Use existing (in-house) technologies first and wireframe the solution at no/low cost • Consider vendor applications if appropriate	Establish a data quality measurement and control framework that does the following: • uses data quality and provisioning status across the firm • explicitly defines data quality metrics, measurements, and benchmarks for analysis and control

Data Management Maturity

Understanding the maturity of a firm's data management capabilities is a useful way to determine operational and technical areas of excellence and improvement. There are many different representations and assessment models of data management maturity. Generally, these models provide a framework for assessing the maturity and institutionalization of data management processes, procedures, quantitative measurements, and incorporation of critical feedback for continuous process and architectural improvements.

Refer to the EDM Council Data Management Capability Assessment Model (*https://edmcouncil.org*) for more detailed information on these models.

Table 7-5 outlines an example of the general maturation phases of a firm's data management operation, beginning with the emergent phase and progressing to the integrated/optimized phase. You should ultimately strive to achieve the state that combines the benefits of a robust data management operation with both data governance and data management/control operations. Robust data governance and data management/control operations are those where data is managed with precision using data governance practices, precise data quality measures, and quantitative data quality metrics.

Disciplined data governance combined with efficient data management and control operations and precisely aligned data architecture generally leads to reductions in data misalignment, data errors, operational issues, and poor decision making based on spurious data.

Table 7-5. Data management maturity model

	Emergent phase	Developing phase	Structured phase	Integrated/Optimized phase	
				Target state Blend and balance data governance and quantitative data quality management to meet business needs and drive continuous improvement in data management operations	
Discipline	Ad hoc activities and simple data onboarding processes	Managed operations using data lifecycle	Repeatable data management operations using data architecture and platforms	Quantitatively managed operations with focus on data governance and data quality	Optimized data management and control using DQS and integrated metrics
Description	Ad hoc, individual efforts, inconsistent processes, not repeatable Individual efforts drive functional performance Limited use of tools	Organized operational function with multiple resources, areas of expertise, and division of labor Critical data flows and processes documented, limited repeatable processes, event-driven data triage and remediation	Organized operational function with multiple resources, areas of expertise, and division of labor Critical data flows and processes are documented, some repeatable processes, event-driven monitoring	Defined statistics and metrics for data quality management Comprehensive processes and procedures with measurements and metrics Metrics used for process and data production control	Focus on quantitative metrics and feedback to optimize processes Center of excellence and domain expertise for continuous improvement in data management operations

Summary

As I hope this chapter made clear, the main purpose of a Data Governance function is to promote and drive a structured, disciplined approach to the management, owner-ship, stewardship, access, and use of data assets. The function drives awareness and recognition of the value of data. It uses the quality metrics about the data and the data management process, to foster continuous improvements in the methods, processes, and architectures used to manage data. Data governance is highly focused on data quality and ensuring that all aspects of data curation are geared to deliver high-quality data for business consumption.

The next chapters return to the concepts of thinking like a manufacturer, the shape of data and data dimensions, and DQS. These concepts and frameworks directly relate to, underpin, and support the goals and objectives of data governance.

CHAPTER 8

Master Data Management

This chapter defines important principles and data structures in master data management architectures used for mastering data volumes. It illustrates the alignment and synergy of data governance and master data management and discusses how they support data quality engineering. I define *master data management* (*MDM*) as the process of establishing and implementing the architectures, standards, processes, policies, and tools used to define and manage critical data in order to provide a single mastered volume of validated, approved, and certified data to business functions across the firm. *Mastering* data means the data is organized into domain-specific volumes where relevant data quality validations and anomaly detection techniques have been used to certify and approve it for use.

The financial industry has recognized the proliferation of highly distributed independent silos of data, and the use of a single, large, centralized data store does not optimally support best practices in data architecture and data management. Instead, the industry recognizes that natural collections of data such as security, reference, holdings, transactions, prices, client accounts, performance, and so on each have unique architecture, quality, and data management requirements for database and file structure implementations, data retention, and data access.

There are many different variations and definitions of master data management, just as there are many different technical and architectural implementations. For more on data engineering, consult *Fundamentals of Data Engineering* by Joe Reis and Matt Housley (O'Reilly). *Data Management at Scale* by Piethein Strengholt (O'Reilly) presents interesting insights and considerations for implementing data architectures, including MDM at scale. And, for a highly detailed presentation of the foundational concepts in master data management and data governance, check out *Master Data Management and Data Governance* (*https://oreil.ly/MzdAS*), by Alex Berson and Larry Dubov (McGraw-Hill).

Mastering Data

MDM for the purpose of data quality engineering relies on two key principles:

1. Data passes from a raw level to a staging level, where data quality is validated using DQS and anomaly detection. Once the data has been validated or remediated, the data is released to the master level.

2. Master-level data is organized into domain-specific data volumes (e.g., security, price, account, holdings) in architectures that contain validated and approved data for distribution and use by downstream consumers.

Therefore, the MDM framework generally requires that data move through three definitive states:

Raw data
> Untouched data; typically the initial instance of data received from a third-party data provider or the raw data expressed from internal applications.

Staged data
> A selection of raw data or the entire raw dataset that is staged for transformation, augmentation, enrichment, rationalization, and assessment of cohesion alignment with other datasets. Data quality of the staged data is evaluated according to the DQS of end consumers and applications. During this stage, data anomaly detection methods and data remediation techniques are used. Data quality metrics are generated based on the tolerances specified in the DQS. This quality control approach is used widely in materials processing and manufacturing.

Mastered data
> The selection of staged data that satisfies the DQS and data quality validations and is considered approved and validated for consumer use. The data is promoted and released to the master data volume.

This process of data movement is agnostic to the technologies used to structure and manage the data volumes. The selection and use of technologies to validate data quality and master data are entirely your decision. However, the technologies may be predominantly driven by the database system, file system, software applications, and programming languages that your firm is most familiar with and commonly uses.

Data volumes used in the financial industry have grown in both diversity and size. This means you must pay increased attention to data definition, standards, and consistency in meaning and use. You may also need to have specialists on your team who understand the data—its use and impact to the business functions, as well as the consumers who use it.

The financial industry generally assumes the data being provided by a vendor or upstream application is valid and ready for use. Yet, we know from experience that data used for different processing specifications is often missing, inaccurate, misshaped, and misaligned to the input expectations and DQS of the consumer. Many times, data issues are discovered *after* use. Then, *reactive* data quality diagnostic techniques are employed, often using reconciliation to assess the data issues and determine data remediation actions. The duplication of data revalidation and reconciliation within multiple business functions is one of the greatest barriers to operational scale and is typically one of the biggest contributors to inefficient operations.

However, in manufacturing, *proactive* quality and specification validation processes are used to test materials entering and moving through the production process. These materials are either already certified for use at the time of delivery, according to specifications and quality standards, or their quality is tested and verified *prior* to introducing the materials to the manufacturing process. Post-manufacturing quality assurance techniques are used to confirm that the materials or manufactured components meet the tolerances and the required specifications *before* distribution to the next manufacturing process or final shipment. There are many quality measures and metrics before, during, and after the production process that drive quality assurance and management functions in manufacturing.

Contemporary MDM processes use the following:

- Hybrid centralized data infrastructures
- Data mastering tools
- Centralized, yet often enterprise-wide in scope, data stewardship and management functions
- Data governance frameworks
- Data glossaries, dictionaries, and inventories
- Standardized data definitions
- Recognized data ownership
- Data usage policies
- Embedded, proactive data quality validation

Like manufacturing, proactive data quality validation in the form of quality assessments—relative to valid and approved tolerance ranges, outlier and anomaly detection, and data quality metrics—has proven to reduce the downstream impact of inaccurate data.

Here are some benefits of using proactive data quality validation:

- Improves operational efficiency by reducing or eliminating redundant data revalidation

- Reduces operational cost by reducing the time and effort spent by consumers revalidating or locally remediating data within downstream applications

- Reduces operational risk due to incorrect data

- Improves the effectiveness of the IT function and its delivery of new functionality and capabilities

- Improves confidence in the data—the data quality satisfies the consumers' DQS and data quality metrics and is within valid business tolerances

- Enables business flexibility and innovation with easy-to-use, high-quality data

MDM and data governance are complementary and, together, are designed to promote a *data-quality-first* culture with comprehensive, quantitatively based data quality management techniques, metrics, and insights to support and help drive business value. The Data Management function and MDM architectures are intended to provide operationally effective, cost-efficient, and strategically enabling capabilities to the business with the support of data governance. MDM architectures use physical data management capabilities, such as databases and data file technologies, to enable the cost-efficient and highly performant use of physical data stores and technical resources. MDM includes delivery of data glossaries and data inventories to promote firm-wide understanding of the data assets that are available for use. A *data glossary* is an easily searchable collection of data elements, definitions, and other metadata about the data you generate and use in your firm. A *data inventory* is also a searchable collection of the physical data volumes and technical details about them, including data classes, data sources, data structures, record counts, data management applications, storage media, and so on. MDM supports data stewards, who perform data remediation and data augmentation with applications and sensors designed to systematically measure data quality, identify anomalies, and generate data quality metrics.

Mastering data is performed in data architectures that support initial data acquisition, quality analysis, remediation and augmentation, and then final mastering and provisioning. Curated, mastered data is preserved according to the firm's needs and is subject to regulatory data retention minimums that support efficient business operations and all necessary audit and transparency requirements. Mastered data is provisioned through data abstraction layers to insulate the firm's business applications from the physical data architecture. *Data abstraction* promotes uniform, controlled, and consistent data provisioning and enables technical flexibility to change and improve data structures in the most cost-efficient and performant means possible.

Enterprise data management (EDM) brings data governance, data quality engineering, and MDM together. EDM is typically an organizational function performed by data stewards who have deep expertise in the relevant classes of data, MDM techniques, data inventory and glossary management, DQS, data validations, data remediation, and data quality analytics. In organizations that practice EDM, data is managed, controlled, and mastered within cost-effective technical architectures and applications to meet the data and data quality needs of the business.

Table 8-1 illustrates the alignment of data governance, master data management, and enterprise data management as a stacked set of capabilities. Data governance spans all capability layers of MDM. EDM works with data governance and information technology and focuses on data definition, inventory, ownership, stewardship, data usage, and most important, data quality assurance.

Table 8-1. MDM stack

Master data management			
Data governance Data definitions Policies and standards Leadership and guidance Data inventories Data project methodology Training	Data access and distribution	**Data access** • Roles- and policy-driven data access	Information Security
		Data distribution • Data abstractions (web services, APIs)	
	Data management	**Data quality assurance** • DQS • Quantitative data quality validations • Anomaly detection and remediation • Data quality measurements and metrics	Enterprise data management Data management and control Data quality expertise
		Data use policy • Defines the approved standard of care when using data in business operations	
		Data ownership and stewardship • Data owners define the DQS • Data stewards manage the data according to the DQS	
	Data inventory	**Data definition and inventory** • Data dictionaries, glossaries, data lineage	
	Physical structures	**Data architecture model** • Data structures (raw, staged, mastered) • Logical data modeling (security, portfolio holding records, and so on), data identification	Information Technology
		Data management technologies • Databases, schemas, tables	

Figure 8-1 illustrates the primary components of an MDM architecture that includes the raw, staged, and mastered data structures as well as data abstraction, data warehouse, and data marts. A data abstraction layer (custom APIs, web services, database views) is used to insulate data consumers from the physical infrastructure. Data governance applies to both the technical infrastructure and business operations. Data stewards in the EDM function typically use a suite of applications to manage data inventories, data quality validations, and data remediation in the MDM architecture.

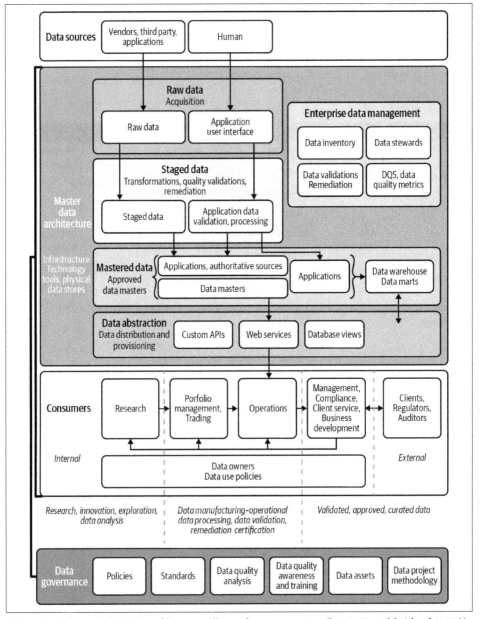

Figure 8-1. Sample MDM architecture (large format version (https://oreil.ly/dqef-8-01))

Data Governance Synergies

As we covered in Chapter 7, data governance is a framework comprised of policies, standards, data inventories, glossaries, ontologies, data lineage, data quality assessments, validations, metrics, and tools that provide business value.

Data governance drives or provides the following:

- Definitions and *authoritative* information about a firm's data assets
- Guidance for the data consumers about *approved* methods of data access and use
- Direction to the data stewards and owners about the *standard of care* for data
- Metrics about the *quality* of the data and its approval for use in business processes
- Consensus about the *criticality* of certain data. Data criticality is assessed based on the degree of business impact to the firm. Data designated as having Critical Data Elements (CDE) typically has the highest business value and the highest business impact if the data is incorrect. The following examples illustrate the implications of incorrect CDE:
  — Misrepresentation to a regulator
  — Misrepresentation to a client
  — Misrepresentation to an auditor
  — Improper, poor, or incorrect operations and management decisions

Let's quickly review some of the key points covered in Chapter 7. The Data Governance function promotes the treatment and recognition of data and information as a valuable, enterprise-wide asset that is fit for purpose and organized in approved data volumes for use by business functions. Business functions use data assets in their processes to provide the highest levels of client services and investment returns possible, to deliver the best insights and investment guidance to clients, and to demonstrate transparency in investment and management decisions. Using validated, high-quality data delivers improved operational efficiency by providing the shape and quality of data aligned to business function DQS, enables compliance with regulatory mandates, enhances audit transparency, and supports prudent risk management. Using high-quality data is also expected to reduce operational risk and cost by reducing or eliminating redundant data processing and duplicative or misaligned data content. Data governance means embedding data stewardship from data discovery and definition all the way through data processing, enrichment, and distribution. Data stewards employ quantitative measurements, metrics, and reporting. Data should be understood, and quality should be measured and verified to certify the data is ready for business use.

A data governance framework and MDM architecture work synergistically together to drive the provisioning and use of the highest quality data based on anticipated benefit and cost and resourcing constraints. Used together, they establish foundational approaches to managing data quality validations. Such approaches include using quantitative metrics to certify that the data meets the business function DQS. A data governance framework and MDM architecture also drive the implementation and use of authoritative data inventories and consistent data definitions as well as the sourcing of validated data from technical architectures. They promote the use of data abstraction layers (e.g., APIs, database views) that enable consistency in data provisioning and consumer use while insulating the firm's business applications and processes from the underlying physical data structures. This affords the IT function the opportunity and flexibility to structure and optimally manage the physical data architecture while minimizing disruptions to the business functions.

The Data Governance function supports MDM by implementing policies that provide guidance about the proper treatment and use of the firm's data and information assets. Data governance, business function data usage, and market data usage are examples of data governance policies. The function promotes the use of industry-recognized standards for metadata, data types, standardized formats, and data element naming conventions. Examples of these standards will be discussed in Chapter 9.

The Data Governance function also monitors data quality relative to the DQS defined by consumers. The function provides data quality awareness training and guidance to institutionalize a data-quality-first approach to stewarding data as a critical asset—one that is most valuable to the operating integrity of your organization and often reflects your firm's intellectual property.

Data governance is also a key contributor to your firm's project and technical development methodologies by ensuring that important data-related activities are included in the overall process.

Data Management Synergies

The EDM function typically comprises one or more teams of data stewards who have expertise managing different classes of data. This function uses the master data architecture to assess the quality of data relative to consumers' DQS. The master data architecture supports the EDM function with data structures, programs, tools, and applications used to identify data anomalies and assess data quality. The EDM function is authorized to perform data remediation to correct and align data to consumers' DQS. The function, in cooperation with data governance, manages the data inventory in the form of data dictionaries, glossaries, data lineage diagrams, and so on that define the physical data stores, data volumes, and approved data access mechanisms in data abstraction layers (web services, custom APIs, and database views).

The EDM function works with data owners, who have the highest level of subject matter expertise about the data and its use. These data owners are typically the direct users of the data and have the authority over decisions about the source, methodology, integrity, and approved use of the data. Owners define the DQS of the data as well as the care and quality requirements for the data to be fit for purpose for a business function or for the firm.

The EDM function may be a centralized, distributed, or hybrid function of data stewards. Collectively, the data stewards are responsible and accountable for the curation of data. *Curation* includes the acquisition, definition and profiling, quality and integrity validation, data error remediation, data quality metrics, preservation, and distribution of the data. Data stewards are responsible for delivering the data fit for purpose, as defined by the consumers' DQS. The data owners typically determine the general standards of data quality, and then the data stewards use the MDM architecture, tools, and applications to curate the data, working in collaboration with IT to deliver the data according to DQS. Within financial firms, data stewards are increasingly organized into centralized teams, creating centers of excellence with data domain expertise and using more centralized data management platforms.

Summary

MDM architectures continue to evolve with the introduction of new technologies and new data management applications. While technologies, data structures, and applications for mastering data are important, what is most important is curated, high-quality data that meets consumers' DQS. This chapter illustrated the three states of data in a master data architecture. The key point is: raw data is held in a staging data structure while the required data quality validations are done, along with any enrichment and transformation activities necessary to confirm that data satisfies consumers' DQS and that the shape of the data aligns with the master data volume. The objective of mastering data in an MDM architecture is to provide a safe data environment to verify data quality, as well as cohesion and collection dimensions, before releasing the data as an approved mastered dataset. The mastered datasets are organized into class-specific data volumes (e.g., security, reference, account, holdings). These master data volumes contain the approved data that is ready for use by you and your business functions.

You can use multiple technologies to validate the DQS, which were defined and illustrated in Chapters 3 and 4. Microsoft Excel can be used to operate on small data volumes, and Python can be used on much larger data volumes. You can also use sophisticated third-party EDM applications, or your firm may have proprietary data structures and programs for data quality validation. Ultimately, your goal is to confirm data quality before the data is released to consumers for use.

The next chapter outlines the activities that are typically defined in a project development methodology. The chapter focuses on important data definition, data integrity, and data management activities that directly relate to data quality, DQS, data governance, and data mastering. These activities give insight into the project tasks and artifacts that you can use to engineer data quality in your data architectures and data processing pipelines.

CHAPTER 9

Data Project Methodology

This chapter presents the *data project methodology* for analytical tasks and artifacts commonly used throughout the lifecycle of data-intensive development projects—from requirements to implementation. Most development projects that support your business will involve implementing new, or modifying existing, data volumes, data structures, and data processing pipelines in architectures and applications that support one or more business functions.

The data project methodology we introduce in this book is not intended to be an exhaustive list of *all* business- and technology-related tasks and artifacts that may be required by a project development methodology or by your firm. Instead, this methodology primarily focuses on important tasks and artifacts that involve comprehensive data analysis and that support the implementation of data governance objectives throughout the data definition, data integrity, and data management project phases.

 Data definition, data quality analysis, implementation of DQS, and data management activities are agnostic to the methodology used in technology development and implementation. Data project methodology tasks and artifacts can be integrated into traditional waterfall methodologies as well as more contemporary Agile and Kanban development frameworks.

The data project methodology illustrated in Figure 9-1 provides a logical progression of tasks and artifacts, beginning with the business use case and processes, understanding the systems and applications involved, and then focusing on the data. The set of tasks labeled "data definitions" are intended to fully describe the data. The set of tasks labeled "data integrity" drive the definition of the DQS and the data quality controls required by the business function and application consumers. The set of tasks labeled "Data Management" focus on the support model that will perform the necessary data monitoring, data management, and data remediation to meet the DQS and the business data requirements.

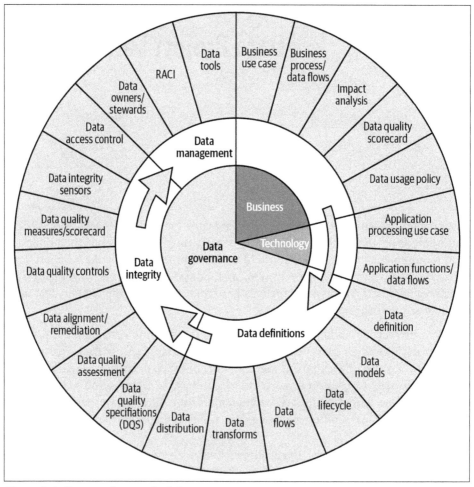

Figure 9-1. Data project methodology

Tasks and artifacts at the data definition, data integrity, and data management stages intend to answer the following three general questions:

1. At the data definition stage: what data is required and for what business purpose?

2. At the data integrity stage: what are the data quality requirements of the business?

3. At the data management stage: once the project is implemented, what is the data management support model that will ensure the data meets defined DQS and business expectations?

These processes, data analysis tasks, and resulting artifacts are intended to reduce data misalignment, minimize data quality misconceptions, and ensure that the data management support model is well defined and viable to both manage data and to deliver the quality of data necessary to meet your business's requirements. The next sections will cover the business, technology, and data governance requirements for a data-intensive project.

Business Requirements

In the financial industry, most data projects represent a response to new or changed requirements initiated by the industry or the business. Your firm may require new types of vendor data to meet new or changed regulatory requirements or to launch new investment products or services. Or your firm may implement new software applications to improve operational processes. In general, most projects in the financial industry have a data component.

This section discusses important data-related activities and artifacts that contribute to defining the business requirements for a data-intensive project.

Defining the Business Use Case

In most data projects, new data and applications are integrated into existing business processes. Defining the project's business use case is an initial step to more fully understanding the data requirements to meet the business need. Business use cases and data usage scenarios tend to illustrate or draw out project requirements.

Further, business professionals are typically unaccustomed to defining the detailed data requirements used in their functions and applications, but they do know what data is used in their business processes and how. They have assumptions and expectations about the end results, benefits, and ramifications on their processes following the implementation. The common phrase "But, I assumed…" tends to result in rework and unhappy consumers. First, define the business use case. It should describe the processes and the data sources, data volumes, and distributions used (or intended for use) by the business function.

Mapping Business Processes and Data Flows

Business process maps and *business flow diagrams* are project artifacts that outline how business processes and business functions align with data, data processing, data transformations, and data validations. Business process maps and flow diagrams include both the current state and future state of a project. A future-state business process map often illustrates data control points and critical processing transformations. This is the initial step toward identifying pre-use data validations and data quality measurements that, combined, form the basis of DQS.

It is important to include data dependencies in the process maps and flow diagrams. Most business processes and applications have upstream data and application dependencies, as well as downstream dependents on the data outputs. The upstream data dependencies or data sources should be fully documented to ensure that any new requirements for data from upstream sources meet the DQS. Similarly, the downstream dependencies or consumers should be fully documented to ensure any new requirements for data intended for distribution meet the consumers' data volumes and DQS requirements.

Impact Analysis

The *business impact of incorrect or misaligned data* is assessed and understood early in the data project methodology. Different data errors have different impacts on the business. Use the business impact definitions, introduced in Chapter 3 and reviewed below, to understand the level of data controls and the data validations that should be implemented during the project. Business impact analysis is primarily focused on critical data elements (CDEs) that represent high-value data; if this data is incorrect, it tends to have a significant negative impact on the business.

The business impact definitions below were covered in Chapter 3 and illustrated in the DQS example in Chapter 4. Impact is either high, medium, or low based on the impact of data errors and poor-quality data that fails to satisfy the DQS of business functions and data consumers:

High impact
> The impact of incorrect data to the business function, consumer, or application could lead to financial data misrepresentation or incorrect decision making. This may result in financial penalties, loss of client trust, regulatory violations, and reputational damage. This data is typically defined as CDE. The business function processes that use the incorrect data are likely in a failure state. The data may be incomplete or inaccurate and may require an immediate response and data remediation, followed by root cause analysis to understand the issues and improve the data quality controls.

Medium impact
> The impact of incorrect data to the business function, consumer, or application results in reduced operational efficiency in the form of wasted resource time. The business function is still operational, but is impaired in some way and unable to fully operate with the incorrect data. Medium-impact data errors typically require triage to determine appropriate data remediation tasks that may include correcting and re-sourcing the data, and rerunning data pipelines. The impact is not considered critical or high. Root cause analysis is likely used to understand the issues and improve the data quality controls.

Low impact

The impact of incorrect data to the business function, consumer, or application is minor and the function is still able to operate with or without the correct data. Low-impact data errors may require triage to understand the root cause, potential data remediation tasks, and improvements in data quality controls. Since the impact is low, further data correction and control improvement activities may be deemed a lower priority.

 The impact analysis of incorrect or poor-quality data on a business function is the basis for the business impact designation in the DQS, at the datum and data volume levels. This analysis is also used to define the RACI (responsible, accountable, consulted, informed) model, discussed later in this chapter, that outlines the functions, tasks, and communications required to manage data issues.

Defining Data Quality Scorecards

Data quality scorecards are periodic reports that reflect the quality metrics of the data used by a business function. The scorecard concept is simple. Data quality is measured and assessed relative to the business function DQS. The definition of the scorecard occurs early in the project, based on the initial understanding of the data and data quality requirements (which result from analysis during the process and data flow mapping and the impact analysis). The detailed development of data quality scorecards happens later in the project lifecycle, when the DQS are defined for the function. We'll discuss scorecards in more detail later in the chapter.

Data Usage Policies

Data usage policies are typically statements about the importance and value of data used in the business function and provide guidance about the expected and approved standard of care for data. The purpose of these types of policies is to promote effective, efficient, and controlled data management, processing, and usage practices within the business function.

The scope of a data usage policy outlines guidance about the following:

- Data-related business processes and operations within the business function
- The use of approved data architectures, databases, data management systems, and data processing applications
- Data provisioning to other functions and applications
- Compliance with information security policies and procedures
- Data quality requirements defined in DQS across data dimensions

- Authorized users, access, and uses of the data both within and external to the function

- Authorized data stewards who have access to the data and perform data remediation activities

- Special data naming conventions and definitions specific to the data used by the function

- Approved storage locations and distribution mechanisms of data used within or generated by the function

- Business-function-specific best practices and standard of care to be applied to data that may include statements about approved and required data sources, volumes, types, formats, precision, accuracy, timing, collection, validations, and so on

At a high level, a data usage policy provides guidance to members of the business function about the approved source, use, storage, and distribution of data—this is aligned with data governance principles. Policies provide insight into how data is used by a business function, thus elucidating data requirements that must be understood, integrated, and satisfied by any new data project.

Technology Requirements

Data lives in technology. Thus, for any data project, there are many requirements analysis tasks and technical artifacts involved. This section talks about two important activities and artifacts that help define the technical data and data flow requirements for a data-intensive project.

Defining the Application Data Processing Use Case

An *application data processing use case* refers to the technical architectures and data processing of the applications used by the business function. Creating new or modifying existing data, architectures, and application functionality for the business is one of the main objectives of a data project. The application data processing use case uncovers technical details about the data source, data volumes, data processing, and distribution components of the applications. These technical details link to the data processes defined in the business use case.

Mapping Application Functions and Data Flows

Application process maps and *data flow diagrams* are project artifacts that outline the data volumes, data sources, inbound data flows, data processing application functions, and outbound data flows. These artifacts show both the current state and future state. Future-state function maps and data flow diagrams illustrate recognizable data requirements, but also facilitate recognition and understanding of other data dependencies—such as reference data and data cohesion requirements—that may not be obvious from the business function perspective. These artifacts provide additional technical details about the data sources, volumes, data sufficiency requirements, and so on that will inform the development of the DQS.

The application process maps and data flow diagrams may contain a broad set of technical details. Here are the important data-related details to include in these artifacts:

- Data sources, inbound data flows, data volumes, generated and derived data, outbound data flows, and data consumers
- Mapping data elements to application functionality
- Rules associated with the shape, format, and quality of the data in the application
- Data validation checks and controls
- Data required for sequencing of operations
- Data relationships between applications
- DQS of the data consumers, using outbound data from the application
- Storage, data structure, and data distribution mechanisms

Application process maps and data flow diagrams reflect the application functions and the data used by the business, as defined in the business process maps and data flows. The technical data flows contain technical details such as data types, data formats, data structures, and so on that you would not find in a business data flow diagram. These technical details inform the development of the DQS, which we'll discuss in the next section.

Data Governance Requirements

Data governance project activities and artifacts are organized into three primary categories:

Data definition tasks
These tasks include defining the data elements, data volumes, collections, and data models.

Data integrity tasks
These tasks include defining the DQS, performing data quality assessments, and defining data quality controls and detailed data quality measures, metrics, and scorecard.

Data management tasks

These tasks include defining data owners and stewards and the data anomaly scenarios in RACI matrices where data remediation is required as part of the data management support model.

Data Definition Tasks

The *data definition* tasks focus on defining the data elements, data collections, and cohesion requirements of the data. These tasks include building data models and detailed data flows, and defining the data lifecycle, data transformations, and data distributions.

Defining data elements and collections

Data definition tasks and artifacts are designed to fully document the data and metadata attributes discussed in Chapter 2, including data element definitions, data types, data collections, data sources, inbound data flows, outbound data distribution flows, transformations, timing requirements, general validations and controls, and user access and permissions. These tasks include developing data dictionaries with complete descriptions of the data elements within the project scope.

Building the data model

The *data model* captures detailed technical requirements, including the data types, data element sizes, whether the data element is mandatory or optional, data precision, and so on. The data model also defines the relationships between the data elements within the project scope and other data volumes. These relationships are often documented as primary and foreign data key relationships that support data cohesion, covered in Chapter 3.

Defining the data lifecycle

The *data lifecycle* reflects the origination or creation, processing, use, transformation, storage, retention, and retirement (archive or deletion) of the data. The data lifecycle details the nature of the data and documents the storage, retention, and retirement rules for the data, based on your organization's policies and regulatory requirements.

Detailing the data flows

The initial *data flow* diagrams developed early in the project organization phase are used as the basis to document the detailed data flows of data elements between and within systems and applications, including data feeds and databases. These flow diagrams include data sources, data sinks, application processing data requirements, user processing data requirements, transformations, storage technologies, data distribution mechanisms, and the DQS of downstream consumers.

Defining the data transformations

Data transformations include data code value translations, calculations, derivations, or the use of industry-standardized values. Data transformations that are translations to other data are captured and documented. These transformations can include the use of industry-standard data such as country codes, currency codes, and classification codes (industry, sector, asset class, and so on). *Calculations* mean the generation of new data elements based on numerical calculations. *Derivations* mean the generation of new data elements based on an algorithm or heuristic (interpolation). *Augmentation* means the generation of new data elements using concatenation or data manipulation that extends one data element to form another data element.

Defining the data distributions

Data distributions are defined by provisioning data in data structures for query access, API access, or extraction in the form of data files or messages intended for downstream distribution to dependent business functions, applications, and data stores.

 Data projects that develop and implement new or modified data that is intended for distribution and use beyond the functions, applications, and consumers within the project scope must also ensure that the quality of the data meets the DQS of the broader consumers. Data projects tend to primarily focus on select objectives and can easily overlook the data and DQS of broader use cases and consumers.

Data Integrity Tasks

The *data integrity* tasks focus on data quality and include defining the DQS, performing data quality assessments and any required data remediation, and defining data quality controls, detailed data quality measures, metrics, and scorecards.

Defining the DQS

The DQS framework introduced in Chapter 3 is used to define the *data quality specifications* and tolerances for data quality validations and verifications. This information is used to embed data quality validations and data controls in the data management and data distribution infrastructure. The DQS define the required data quality for data dimensions for each data element within the project scope. The DQS are the key to engineering data quality and are a critically important artifact defined in the data project methodology. The DQS are the basis for creating data quality validation controls and data quality measurements of the metrics generated from the application of data quality validation controls. DQS are also the basis for defining the

RACI (responsible, accountable, consulted, informed) matrix, which informs the data management support model.

Performing data quality assessments

A *data quality assessment* is an analysis exercise to determine the quality of the existing data to be used within the scope of the project. The future-state data quality requirements are documented, indicating the data quality of the expected data along with any gaps in the shape or quality of the data required by the project. Determining a fit-for-purpose level is an integral part of this analysis. Data in source systems is often assumed to be fit for purpose for use by the business function or applications within the project scope. However, given that the data and functionality in a project tend to change, the data must be revalidated for fit-for-purpose levels to confirm whether the data and its quality will satisfy the new or modified target systems, applications, and business requirements.

It is almost always the case that data that originally satisfied a business function's requirements will fall short of new project requirements. Analyzing the data quality of source systems and the current data within scope of the project is required to understand if there are any data and data quality gaps. If such gaps are found, then data upgrades, data remediation, and additional data quality validations and controls must be added as requirements to the scope of the project.

This analysis, and resulting project tasks and activities, will reduce data misalignment issues and minimize the risk of unknown data gaps that could affect the project. The goal of a data project is to achieve optimal alignment of business processes, user interactions, and the data volumes to meet the business objectives. This analysis is intended to minimize the risk of unknown data gaps or misaligned data issues that could impact or derail the project.

Performing data realignment and remediation

The data quality assessment is used to determine which tasks are required to augment, realign, and clean up data in order to meet the new project requirements and DQS. The operational data stewards, who are responsible for the source data and supporting the consumers' DQS, execute on the data augmentation, enhancement, or remediation tasks. They develop and establish the standard operating procedures, use data validation tools, and remediate any data errors that would affect the new DQS of the business function or consumers' applications. This assessment also includes defining the pre-use data validations upon generation of data that is intended for distribution, based on the downstream consumer DQS.

Defining and implementing data quality controls

Data validation controls are primary, pre-use data validations that are implemented as systematic programs that measure the applicable data dimensions of each datum relative to their tolerances defined in DQS. They test the quality and integrity of the data being used, generated, and distributed. Data quality controls are required to ensure each datum in a data volume meets the consumers' DQS. Data validations should be used as pre-use, primary controls to ensure the data is ready for distribution to the downstream consumers or stored in master data volumes for general consumption *before* the data is used or distributed.

Data verification controls are secondary, post-use data validations that are implemented as systematic programs prior to or in the consumer's applications. Data verifications validate that data received from upstream sources satisfies the DQS of the consumer. The data verification metrics indicate whether the data aligns with the consumers' DQS, is free from any data anomalies, and is ready for use. If data verification tolerances are breached, then there are issues and errors in the data that mean the upstream primary data controls should be reviewed to determine the gap in data quality and root cause. Data in the upstream source can fulfill DQS prior to distribution, but there may be newly introduced application or system processing logic that results in inconsistencies or bugs in data queries, APIs, and data transmission logic, which can then result in malformed data being provided to downstream consumers.

You use data validations as primary controls to confirm whether the data is fit for purpose according to DQS. You use data verifications as secondary controls to confirm whether the data you received still meets the DQS. This primary and secondary control framework is helpful to triage both the data and the technologies involved in the data ecosystem or pipeline when data anomalies and errors are detected between systems, architectures, and applications.

Measuring and scorecarding data quality

Data quality measurements, based on DQS, generate data quality metrics that indicate whether the quality of the data is within or exceeding acceptable tolerances. *Scorecarding data quality*, which we introduced in Chapter 5, means charting and graphing the data quality metrics to demonstrate the following:

- The data is fit for purpose relative to the business function DQS
- The historical quality patterns of the data, which may provide insight into changes in the integrity and quality of data over time
- The acceptable tolerances for each measurement of a data dimension for each data element under inspection

- The statistics about current and past trends of data volumes that typically include the number of datum values, data elements, and records, along with dates, times, or date ranges and the timing of the DQS validation processes

Data quality scorecards provide insight into the quality of each datum. When data quality metrics are presented in a graphical visualization, hierarchies of data quality metrics (valid, suspect, invalid) provide insight into larger data volumes. Comparing real data quality metrics to the acceptable tolerances defined in DQS will show the prevalence of data anomalies and outliers that require further inspection and, potentially, data remediation.

Data integrity sensors

Data quality validation programs are sensors in the data ecosystem—like sensors used in manufacturing to measure production and assembly line operations. Data integrity sensors, or programs, test the data quality based on DQS before the data is used. These sensors operate as follows:

- The programs are implemented as pre-use, data integrity and quality validations prior to the data being used by a business function, consumer, or application.
- The programs are implemented as post-use, data integrity and quality verifications after the data is used, but before the data is distributed further to downstream architectures, systems, and applications.
- Status monitoring is used to provide operational data statistics and data quality metrics that are used to generate data quality scorecards and operational dashboards.
- Data quality alerts are generated by critical data quality tolerance failures from pre-use or post-use data integrity checks. Alerting is also used to notify the Data Management and IT functions about failure conditions and systematic errors.

Ensuring proper access controls

Controlling access to data often requires adhering to information security policies. Generally, data should be provisioned to users, groups, and applications on a *need-to-know* basis, where that data is required to perform specific, approved business functions. You are encouraged to consult with your Information Security function and ensure your data access controls adhere to your firm's data access and data usage policies.

Data Management Tasks

The Data Management function can be organized into many different structures with a diverse set of tasks and activities, but it is generally comprised of data stewards. Data stewards, whether organized as a centralized or decentralized function (or located with IT or other business functions) manage and use data. You can find many variations of this type of function across different organizations. However, regardless of organization structure, data stewards focus on managing data and delivering the highest quality data for business use. There are several important activities in the data project methodology that promote and establish a clear understanding of data owners, data stewards, data remediation responsibilities, and viability of the tools used to operate on the data.

Defining data owners, stewards, and custodian

Data is managed, used, and governed by many functions across a firm. Each business function may have individuals who are data owners, or data stewards, or both. The classification of data owner versus data steward is intentionally simple—it is easy to understand who does what with respect to data. This distinction is very helpful when discussing data quality with business functions that know the quality of the data they need, but do not have the skills to manage and curate the data. Similarly, data stewards understand that their role is to manage the data and its quality to satisfy the data owner's DQS.

Data owners, introduced in Chapter 8, are typically business functions or individuals who have the highest level of subject matter expertise about the data based on experience and industry-recognized certifications. They are often the direct consumers and users of the data, and have authority over decisions about preferred data sources, data quality tolerances to satisfy DQS, and delineation between approved and unapproved uses of the data.

Data owners typically define the tolerances found in DQS that reflect the standards of care and quality and the requirements for the data to be fit for purpose for use by a function or by the firm. Data owners typically do not manage the data or have operational responsibility for the curation of the data. They are considered to be the client for whom the data should be provisioned in accordance with the DQS.

Data stewards are individuals in business functions, or members of a Data Management function, who are devoted to and responsible and accountable for the curation of the data. Curation, as we discussed in Chapter 8, includes the acquisition, definition and profiling, quality and integrity validation, data error remediation, metrics and scorecarding, preservation, and distribution of the data. Data stewards are responsible to deliver the data fit for purpose as defined by the DQS. The data owners will often determine the general tolerances and standards for data quality, and the data stewards apply data curation techniques working in collaboration with Information Technology to deliver the data according to the DQS. Teams of data stewards are increasingly centralized within financial firms due to economies of scale and centralization of data expertise and data management platforms.

The *data custodian* is the IT function. Its purpose is to provide the safe, secure, and performant technical architectures and infrastructure required to support the ingestion, validation, and distribution of data. IT is responsible for the integrity of the technical infrastructure, including applications that store, process, transform, and distribute data across enterprise applications and the data management infrastructure.

The IT function, while responsible for the technical infrastructure, is generally not responsible for the integrity of the data and information. IT is responsible for all technical architecture and applications that may create data errors by design or by bugs in code, or due to failures in technical appliances required by data stewards to manage data and data quality to satisfy DQS.

 It is important to define the data owners and data stewards for all the data elements and volumes within the scope of the project. *There are times when the data owner is also the data steward.* This occurs often in the Data Management function related to vendor data products and data feeds where Data Management has the deepest expertise and the responsibility to curate the vendor data for business consumers. Assigning these roles is highly recommended before reviewing the RACI matrix that will outline who performs which tasks and who needs to be informed when data quality tolerances are breached, and data triage and remediation is required.

Defining the responsibility assignment matrix (RACI)

The RACI (responsible, accountable, consulted, informed) matrix, as we've discussed in earlier chapters, is a highly effective tool that provides clarity about the function and related teams that are responsible for responding to and addressing data quality tolerance issues. The RACI matrix designates which functions or teams may be consulted for expertise or apprised of the data issues and impact to business operations.

The RACI matrix embodies the salient information about data applications, data volumes, data quality tolerances, data quality breaks, and remediation activities. It clearly defines who has the responsibility to manage the data issue, who is accountable for the data controls in data management, who should be consulted, and who should be informed.

Table 9-1 shows the functions and roles that are responsible and accountable for managing different types of critical data quality issues. It also shows the functions that are consulted or informed in the event of one or more data quality issues.

Table 9-1. Example RACI matrix

Condition	Alerts/actions	Remediation	Responsible	Accountable	Consulted	Informed
Empty account number	Completeness alert	Request account number from Client Service.	Client Service	Data Management	Operations Client Service	Client Service
Unknown transaction code	Conformity alert	Research the code; update with the proper transaction code.	Operations	Data Management	Operations	Operations
Incorrect market value	Congruence alert	Research portfolio holdings, transactions, quantity adjustments, and prices. Determine the error and update with the correct market value.	Operations	Operations	Accounting Administrator Trading	Trading Compliance Performance Reporting

Collaboration between data stewards, data owners, business functions, Data Management, and IT on the development and use of RACI matrices is highly valuable and directly supports the success of a project. You are encouraged to create your own RACI matrices and add other important information to the matrix that further enhances its usefulness to your data management and business functions.

Certifying data remediation tools

The data stewards who are responsible for the integrity of the data require data management tools and workflow utilities that support the function. These tools may be specific data quality validation programs or may be comprehensive EDM platforms that enable data stewards to perform validations and remediation. The data management validation and data remediation tools must be reviewed and certified that they can support the new or modified data and data remediation requirements developed and implemented by the project.

New classes of data or new data quality validation logic may not be supported by the existing data management programs and applications. Therefore, enhancements to these tools must be included in the project to support viable data management operations. You can use the RACI matrix as a basis to outline the test cases and data validation scenarios that will exercise the tools for each data error condition. This approach provides immediate feedback on the viability of the data management tools expected to be used after the project goes live. The results of this testing and any required tooling enhancements can also be recognized as prerequisites to final project signoffs and production releases.

Data management tools are critically important to the data stewards who have the responsibility of responding to and addressing data anomalies and errors. If the existing tools cannot be used by the data stewards to perform their tasks, then IT (i.e., the data custodian) is typically the backup set of resources to make data updates and perform data remediation. That scenario is not ideal and results in impaired data management support. It also redirects and drains the IT function's resources.

Summary

Application and project development methodologies tend to focus on the design, development, and selection of technical infrastructures, tools, applications, vendor solutions, and so on. The data project methodology, on the other hand, is designed to focus on all aspects of the data within the project scope. It outlines the important data-related activities that support project implementation best practices regardless of the technologies and development methodologies used. The artifacts developed during these activities include data dictionaries, data flows, DQS, data quality validation programs, data quality scorecards, and RACI matrices. These artifacts are the keys to engineering data quality into your data architectures and data processing pipelines.

Table 9-2 provides a quick reference and summary guidance about the level of detail recommended for the data project tasks and artifacts based on the complexity of the data requirements within the scope of the project. The number of new or modified data elements delineating simple versus complex is subjective. You can use and enhance this methodology template and determine the number that best aligns with your firm's understanding of a simple versus complex data project.

Simple data complexity means a small number (less than 50) of new or modified data elements, or simply structured data volumes, is used in existing, well-understood business processes, data pipelines, and data quality tolerances.

Complex data complexity means a large number (more than 50) of new or modified data elements, or multiple complex data volumes across multiple applications, is used in new and existing business processes with new data pipelines and new data quality validations.

This table is a general guide to the level of detail recommended for each data project task and artifact. Your firm will likely have more specific requirements.

Table 9-2. Data project methodology summary guidance (○ refers to abbreviated details and ● refers to full details)

Domain	Task/artifact	Data complexity scale	
		Simple	Complex
Business	Business use case	●	●
	Business process/data flows	○	●
	Impact analysis	●	●
	Data quality scorecards	●	●
	Data usage policies	○	●
Technology	Application processing use case	○	●
	Application functions and data flows	○	●
Data governance			
Data definition	Data elements and collections	●	●
	Data model	○	●
	Data lifecycle	○	●
	Data flows	○	●
	Data transformations	○	●
	Data distributions	○	●
Data integrity	Data quality specifications (DQS)	●	●
	Data quality assessment	●	●
	Data realignment and remediation	●	●
	Data quality controls	●	●
	Data quality measurement/scorecard	●	●
	Data integrity sensors	●	●
	Data access controls	●	●
Data management	Data owners and stewards	●	●
	Data management RACI matrix	●	●
	Data management tools	●	●

The next and final chapter brings all the components of data quality engineering together in the form of enterprise data management. Understanding your data, measuring data quality, and delivering data that is fit for purpose to your business functions is the primary objective.

CHAPTER 10

Enterprise Data Management

Enterprise data management (*EDM*), introduced in Chapter 8, refers to an organization's capabilities to effectively define, acquire, integrate, manage, and use data and information assets in applications and business processes. EDM delivers business value by combining best practices in data governance, contemporary data architectures, master data management, data quality engineering, and data management operations. This synergy yields the following:

- Increased awareness of the importance and the value of data as an information asset
- Embedded understanding of the data and quality required to drive efficient operations
- Mastered data that ensures data has been validated and approved prior to its use
- Consistency, efficiency, and scale in data management and control
- Standardization in data quality tolerance validations and data quality analytics
- Recognized data ownership and data stewardship roles and responsibilities

EDM exists to promote a data-quality-first culture that enables you and your firm to achieve business strategy goals and objectives. It includes all the methods, techniques, and frameworks presented in this book. I encourage you to use, extend, and enhance them in ways that best align to your firm's business objectives and that can make the most positive impact on how you manage data and drive data quality.

You can use EDM to improve your:

- Understanding of the shape and dimensions of data and data volumes
- Data-wrangling skills with greater insight into the quality and dimensionality of data

- Business functions' abilities to define high-quality data for efficient operations
- Firm's ability to effectively manage data, adhering to quantitative data quality tolerances
- Ability as a data owner to specify data quality tolerances for data stewards
- Ability as a data steward to implement precise, pre-use data quality validations
- Data platforms using pre-use validations and an MDM framework
- Management operation, using data volume statistics and data quality metrics
- Capacity to validate data volumes and detect data anomalies at scale
- Governance of data using policies, procedures, glossaries, and specifications

You may think this sounds like a lot of work. Yes, applying manufacturing principles and precision to data management *can* result in a lot of work, but it is well worth it. At times, it can even be a tedious and mind-numbing journey through the morass of data volumes riddled with scary data anomalies that lack the data curation discipline presented in this book. However, many business professionals and data practitioners who work with data in the financial industry have grown accustomed to working around misshaped and malformed data, incorrect data, missing data, imprecise data, and so on. I believe the financial industry can learn from manufacturing and do a better job managing and delivering high-quality, fit-for-purpose data to its consumers going forward. The good news is that, by now, you have the tools to do just that, with your enlightened understanding of data and data dimensions.

Where to Begin?

There is a great quote by Mark Watney, the character who is stranded on Mars in the movie *The Martian*:

> You just begin. You do the math. You solve one problem and you solve the next one and then the next. And if you solve enough problems, you get to come home.

You begin engineering data quality into your individual data usage processes, business function data pipelines, or the firm's use of data by selecting one problem to solve. Then, move on to the next problem. You take the first step by thinking about data as physical volumes of high-value raw materials and using the DQS tools to understand, define, and measure data dimensions and data quality. You can use the results of your data quality analyses to inform and enrich the definitions of your data and specify the required data quality tolerances that you can share with your colleagues, data stewards, and the Data Management function.

Understanding Data Volumes

As we've discussed, the most common data volumes used in the financial industry are panel data collections (time series cross-sections). Revisit Chapter 2 for information about the shape of data. Do you know the source, structure, data types, definitions, and statistics for each datum in the data volumes you are using? If not, then you can ask for that information to better understand the shape and structure of the data. You can also generate those details about the data for your own use, and you can provide them to data consumers so they can understand the data with greater insight. You can use data dictionaries, glossaries, and inventories to catalog data attributes, elements, and data volumes. You can count datum values and records and determine the date ranges of time series data. You can understand which data volumes are required by business processes, data pipelines, and applications.

If you've made it this far, it should be clear *why* you need to know these details and how necessary and important they are when determining the required data quality tolerances for the data you use to do your job.

Engineering Data Quality

DQS, defined in Chapter 3, provide the framework to measure specific data dimensions of data in data volumes. *Data quality engineering* is the intersection of science and mathematics applied to physically analogous properties (dimensions) of data to measure quality relative to a specification. The DQS examples we've shown demonstrate that you can measure data dimensions and use the metrics to identify data anomalies while confirming that the remaining datum values in the data volume are within acceptable tolerances. Do you receive a data quality scorecard about your data from an internal Data Governance function, Data Management function, or data vendors? If not, then you can ask for that information to better understand the quality of the data you are about to buy or the data that you are using in your data pipelines and applications.

The precise control specifications and quality standards of raw materials used and products produced in the manufacturing industry have been improved and codified over a long period of time. DQS, like control specifications, make up a systematic and quantitative framework that can be applied to data volumes to measure the quality of every datum in the volume. Thanks to your work going through this book, you now have the tools to specify the quality standards, at the datum level, that are required for the use of data by consumers and in your applications.

Improving Efficiency

Time is money. Your time as an employee is precious, and your company pays you to do your job. Yet, everyone seems to know when their time is being wasted chasing data issues instead of getting the real work done. If this sounds familiar, then that is a problem to solve. The DQS framework gives you the tools to convey, design, and implement pre-use data quality validations for your data. If you are a data owner, you can define these tolerances for the data you use or the data that is used by your business function and in your applications. You can share your DQS with your upstream data providers. If you are a data steward, you can ask your data consumers about their tolerances at a detailed level so you can implement pre-use data quality validations for them. Chapter 6 showed the costs and benefits of using pre-use data validations versus reconciliation as primary data controls. Remember the cow example?

Spending your time doing your job with fit-for-purpose, high-quality data positively contributes to operational efficiency. Spending your time chasing incorrect data or working around malformed data does not. However, there are other more serious implications of poor-quality data, such as incorrect decision making, compliance failures, incorrect client reports, and so on. These events can lead to regulatory findings, financial penalties, loss of clients, and in some cases, employees may lose their jobs. This is serious stuff and, as an industry, we have the opportunity to raise the bar when it comes to the quality of the data we use to manage trillions of dollars of other people's wealth. Keep in mind that if you participate in any direct or retirement investment vehicles, such as a 401(k), and hold mutual funds or other managed investments, it is also about *your money* as well. If you are spending time dealing with data issues rather than performing your job function, you have an opportunity to use these tools and demonstrate how better-quality data can yield improvements in your effectiveness and efficiency.

Scaling Data Architectures and Pipelines

Modifying embedded, legacy data structures is very difficult, if not almost impossible. Firms in the financial industry have built extensive data infrastructures over a long period of time. Many of the legacy architectures and data applications that were built years ago using older technologies are failing to meet the new, diverse, and ever-expanding data requirements of the industry today. In addition, the size and scale of data volumes that the financial industry consumes continue to increase and outpace the capacity of human capital to properly manage data using discordant data identification standards, reconciliation reports, and haphazard data quality techniques. Chapter 8 provided an MDM framework for designing and constructing new data architectures that enable the integration of pre-use data quality validations and anomaly detection *at scale*. There is no single human checking each can of Coca-Cola

---

coming off the production line, and likewise, no team of data management professionals has the capacity to individually validate every critical datum by hand.

MDM architectures combined with pre-use data quality validations and exception-based anomaly detection are akin to large-scale, assembly-line manufacturing and production. You can transform and migrate the data processing pipelines that are still using monolithic, brittle data structures over to MDM architectures and integrate the data quality sensors required to deliver high-quality data. The opportunities for these migrations often come when the legacy infrastructure has literally run out of time and can no longer support the business, or when taking a strategic view of the future data needs of the business and undergoing a major transformation initiative. In either case, you can move toward MDM and systematic data quality management to improve the scale at which you and your firm are able to consume and validate data prior to business consumption. Recall from Chapter 5 that while you should be interested in all data quality metrics, you should be *most* interested in those metrics that indicate approaching tolerance or out-of-tolerance conditions (i.e., data anomalies). If you use a comprehensive set of data quality validations that sufficiently defines the acceptable tolerances for data quality, then you can systematically and quantitatively validate all datum in the critical data volumes that your business needs.

Achieving a Data-Quality-First Culture

You can achieve a successful data-quality-first culture in your firm through partnership and collaboration. Data quality is not solely your responsibility, or that of data stewards or the Data Management function. Instead, it is everyone's responsibility. Everyone benefits from working together in cooperation to precisely define, validate, manage, and use high-quality data. Establishing a data-quality-first culture requires partnership between data owners and data stewards from all business and technical functions. And it requires a collective, shared commitment to improving your data management architectures and discipline. Data quality issues, from the simple to the complex, are problems that are best solved by working together. You achieve a data-quality-first culture when you choose to solve a data quality problem and work together using these tools to design and implement the solution. Then, choose the next problem.

Making It Happen

Restructuring data architectures, implementing data quality validations, and establishing a data-quality-first culture in an organization does not happen overnight. Chapter 7 outlined data governance initiatives that raise awareness and understanding through training about the definitions and dimensions of data and the importance of data quality. Data governance provides the guidance to establish the policies and practices to promote the care and treatment of data as a high-value asset.

Chapter 9 introduced the methodology to implement data projects from the early phases of defining the business use case and technical data requirements, through data definition and data integrity, to implementation in the data management phase.

You now have a roadmap, tools, and templates that you can use to define the shape and structure of data volumes, engineer pre-use data quality validations, measure data quality using metrics, identify data anomalies, and clearly define the roles and responsibilities to deliver data that is understood, where quality is measured and the data is fit for purpose for business use. It really is all about the data.

The next chapter is yours, and your journey begins by choosing the first problem to solve.

Data quality engineering begins with you.

Index

quality of data (see data quality; DQS)

R
RACI (responsible, accountable, consulted, informed) matrix, 109, 140
raw data, 118
reactive data quality diagnostic techniques, 119
reconciliation of data, 98-99
    as reactive technique, 119
    compared to pre-use data validation, 99-101
    cost of, 95-96
Reis, Joe
    Fundamentals of Data Engineering, 117
Research function, model of, 46
responsible, accountable, consulted, informed (RACI) matrix, 109, 140
revalidation of data, 119, 136

S
S (suspect) tolerance code, 23
scaling data architectures, 148
Schwartz, Baron
    Anomaly Detection for Monitoring, 5
scorecarding data quality, 131, 137
security attribute, 17
security master data volume, 47, 66, 81
security of data, 17, 104, 138
shape of data, 8-14
Smart Process Plants (Bagajewicz), 5
staged data, 118
standard deviation, comparison to, 39-41, 62-66
standard of care for data, 123
steward attribute, 17
stewards
    attribute for, 17
    defining, 104, 105
    in RACI matrix, 141
    role of, 111, 120-121, 124-125, 136, 139-140
Strengholt, Piethein
    Data Management at Scale, 117

T
technology requirements, 132-133
temporal dimensionality of data, 7
temporal panel data volumes, 26

three-dimensional charts, 89-91
time series cross-section, 11
time series data, 9
timeliness dimension, 17
    DQS example for, 50-52
    tolerances for, 25-27
tolerance codes, 23
    accuracy dimension, 27-30, 52-55
    cohesion dimension, 42-43, 72-77
    collection dimension, 41-42, 67-72
    completeness dimension, 24-25, 48-50
    conformity dimension, 32-33, 58-60
    congruence dimension, 33-41, 60-67
    precision dimension, 30-32, 55-58
    timeliness dimension, 25-27, 50-52
Trading function, model of, 46, 96-97, 99
triangulation, 29
type attribute, 16

U
ultrapure water, 4
univariate time series, 9
universe, 9
use cases
    application data processing use case, 132
    business use case, 129
    DQS based on, 6, 21

V
V (valid) tolerance code, 23
validation of data (see data quality validations)
visualizations of data quality metrics, 82
    heatmaps, 83-89
    three-dimensional charts, 89-91
volumes (see data volumes)

W
water purification, 3
water quality specifications, 4-5
Wilke, Claus O.
    Fundamentals of Data Visualization, 82
Womack, Jim, 2

Z
z-score, comparison to, 39-41, 62-66

About the Author

Brian Buzzelli is senior vice president and head of data governance for Acadian, a quantitative institutional asset management firm specializing in active global, emerging, and frontier investments utilizing sophisticated analytical models and specialized research expertise. Brian has defined a systematic and rigorous approach to data quality engineering through application of manufacturing principles and based on his expertise developed over 27 years of experience. His leadership implementing data governance, data usage policies, data standards, data quality measurement, data taxonomies, architecture, and metadata have supported some of the most complex financial business functions at Acadian, Nomura, Thomson Reuters, and Mellon Financial. Data quality engineering, data management, and the application of manufacturing principles to data dimensions and data quality validation are at the center of his professional focus. He is a graduate of Carnegie Mellon University with a bachelor of science degree in information and decision systems and holds two master's degrees: management of information systems and MBA in finance from the Katz Business School at the University of Pittsburgh.

Colophon

The animal on the cover of *Data Quality Engineering in Financial Services* is a barred spinefoot (*Siganus doliatus*), also known as the two-barred rabbitfish.

The barred spinefoot is found across a tropical swath of the western Pacific Ocean, near Indonesia and Australia, where it lives and feeds in shallow waters around reefs and in lagoons. Like all rabbitfish, it is diurnal, sleeping in reef crevices at night and exhibiting greater activity during the day, when, as a herbivore, it feeds primarily on algae.

Mature individuals of the species are often found in pairs, a behavior likely employed as a protective measure against predation while feeding. An array of venomous spines lining their dorsal and anal fins lends them further protection and has contributed to one of their common designations ("spinefoot"), as have the two dark stripes ("two-barred") running along their oblong, yellow-and-blue bodies.

The barred spinefoot has been categorized by the IUCN as being of least concern, though its dependence on threatened reefs as a habitat has led some conservation scientists to infer possible unobserved population declines. Many of the animals on O'Reilly covers are endangered; all of them are important to the world.

The cover illustration is by Karen Montgomery, based on an antique line engraving from *Fishes of India*. The cover fonts are Gilroy Semibold and Guardian Sans. The text font is Adobe Minion Pro; the heading font is Adobe Myriad Condensed; and the code font is Dalton Maag's Ubuntu Mono.

O'REILLY®

Learn from experts.
Become one yourself.

Books | Live online courses
Instant Answers | Virtual events
Videos | Interactive learning

Get started at oreilly.com.